URBAN DESIGN:
ORNAMENT AND DECORATION

URBAN DESIGN: ORNAMENT AND DECORATION

Cliff Moughtin, Taner Oc and Steven Tiesdell

Institute of Planning Studies, Department of Architecture and Planning
University of Nottingham

Butterworth Architecture
An imprint of Butterworth-Heinemann Ltd
Linacre House, Jordan Hill, Oxford OX2 8DP

 A member of the Reed Elsevier group

OXFORD   LONDON   BOSTON
MUNICH   NEW DELHI   SINGAPORE   SYDNEY
TOKYO   TORONTO   WELLINGTON

First published 1995

British Library Cataloguing in Publication Data
Moughtin, J. C.
  Urban Design: Ornament and Decoration
  I. Title
  711.4

ISBN 0 7506 0792 0

Library of Congress Cataloguing in Publication Data
Moughtin, Cliff
  Urban design:ornament and decoration/Cliff Moughtin, Taner Oc,
  Steven Tiesdell.
  p.   cm.
  Includes bibliographical references and index.
  ISBN 0 7506 0792 0
  1. Urban beautification.   2. Art, Municipal.   I. Oc, Taner, 1944-
  II. Tiesdell, Steven.   III. Title.
NA9052.M68   1995   94-47287
729-dc20   CIP

Composition by Scribe Design, Gillingham, Kent
Printed in Great Britain

CONTENTS

PREFACE

Attitudes to the embellishment of cities with ornament and decoration range from a puritanical iconoclasm that sees such embellishment as decadent and pernicious, to one of joyous pleasure in the experience of complex, intricate and extravagant patterning. The Modern Movement in architecture, epitomized by the writings of Le Corbusier, the pronouncements of CIAM, the work of the Bauhaus and the much criticized post Second World War city developments in Europe, North America and elsewhere, was a time when decoration in architecture was eschewed.

We are now experiencing an attempt to rehumanize our cities aesthetically as well as tackling their social and economic problems. In this book we have adopted an aesthetic approach to urban design, primarily because this is an area that has recently been neglected in the literature. There is a need to discuss the principles that have governed ornament and decoration in cities to guide current efforts to heal and humanize our cities making them more delightful experiences. Sir Henry Wootton described the fundamental qualities of architecture as 'firmness, commodity and delight'. Over the past few decades we have concentrated on the first two criteria. It is therefore timely that we return and explore 'delight'.

In many cities, the city centre streets are being reclaimed from cars and the tarmac replaced with intricate and expensive floorscaping for traffic-calmed streets, but this has not always been successful. Most cities are making an effort to have sculptures in their squares or decorative fountains but few of these are as memorable as the statue of Marcus Aurelius in the Campidoglio or the Trevi Fountain. Thus, it is necessary to identify the principles for the successful embellishment of our cities before we make further mistakes. This book is written to help architects, urban designers, planners, city politicians, developers and citizens in their effort to re-humanize and heal our cities with the assistance of ornament and decoration.

ACKNOWLEDGEMENTS

This book is the second volume in the Urban Design series written at the Institute of Planning Studies. The demanding task of preparing the manuscript was made much easier by the assistance with typing given by Linda Francis and Sarah Shaw, proof reading by Jenny Chambers and illustrations prepared by Peter Whitehouse and Steven Thornton-Jones.

All illustrations and photographs are the authors own with the following exceptions which we would like to acknowledge: Figures 4.4-4.7, by courtesy of the San Francisco Planning Department, redrawn by Steven Tiesdell; Figure 4.9 engraving by Martin Englebrecht; Figure 4.16 perspective by J. H. Aronson, from *Design of Cities* by Edmund Bacon (1974), used by permission of Penguin, a division of Penguin Books USA Inc.; Figure 7.11 by permission of Alastair Gardner, School of Architecture, University of Nottingham; Figures 7.13 and 7.14 by kind permission of Mr J. P. Lenclos.

THEORY AND PHILOSOPHY OF ORNAMENT AND DECORATION

1

INTRODUCTION

Urban design, the art of city building, is concerned with the methods used to organize and structure the urban realm as distinct from the detailed design of the private domain. This book deals with one aspect of urban design: the role, function and form of ornament and decoration in the city. The book is written from the perspective that all development should be judged as an attempt to decorate the city. Alexander has suggested that each increment of development should aim to 'heal' or make 'whole' the city (Alexander, 1987). The thesis presented here accepts this notion but advocates the primacy of ornament and decoration in the process of unifying parts of the city into comprehensive wholes. The thesis that each increment of development should be seen as an attempt to decorate the city does not conflict with the idea that urban development results from consideration of such practical matters as function, use, cost, economic location and available finance: the city would stagnate and die without due consideration being given to these prerequisites of development. However, having solved the practicalities of development, the ultimate criterion for evaluating any addition to the city is whether that increment decorates the city.

Ornament and decoration, when used to heal the city has three interrelated functions. They are: to go beyond the decoration of individual buildings and to enrich the decorative themes of a locality; to enhance the physical, social and spiritual qualities of location, that is, to strengthen the genius loci, and thirdly to develop the 'legibility' and 'imageability' of the city. Prior to the twentieth century, the conscious effort to decorate was an intrinsic part of large scale development (Figure 1.1). In the twentieth century, with exceptions, it would appear the primacy of decoration has been replaced in urban development by other, mainly economic interests. It may be that we have to look back to the past to rediscover the rationale for decoration. Without such a rationale, decoration and ornament in the city may be seen as fussy, precious and florid, a veneer to cover cheap and shoddy development.

For the purpose of this book, ornament and decoration will be taken to mean the ways in which the main elements within the city are arranged to form a pleasing and memorable pattern. The analysis of ornamentation and decoration in the city will be structured around Lynch's notion of urban legibility (Lynch, 1960). The text will therefore be based upon the five components Lynch suggested as being key to imageability: the path, the node, the edge, the

Figure 1.1 Decorative railings, Nancy

landmark and the district. The legible city, that is, the city easily visualized in the 'minds eye' has, according to Lynch, a clearly defined, easily recognized and distinctive perceptual structure. To a certain degree the reading or understanding of a city is personal but with a clearly structured city, the result, it is argued, is a city population with a shared set of images. It is this shared image which is one of the concerns of urban design. This book explores the possibility for ornament and decoration to emphasize and clarify the five components and so strengthen the city's image and enhance its attraction for citizen and visitor.

The two words 'decoration' and 'ornament' appear in the title of this book. According to the *Shorter Oxford English Dictionary*, both words have a similar meaning: embellishment. Decoration, however, has everyday associations: one decorates the home, the living room, the Christmas tree, or the wedding cake. Ornament, on the other hand, has more formal overtones: the ornamental work associated with certain architectural styles or the work of individual architects. This book accepts this subtle difference in meaning and uses ornament to mean the installation of sculpture, fountains, obelisks and similar features into the urban scene. Decoration is used to describe populist activities such as the placing of gnomes in the front garden, topiary work or decorating the city for festivals such as Christmas and Diwali. Obviously there are large areas of overlap: a precise boundary between formal ornamentation and informal decoration is not possible, nor indeed, would it be desirable.

Camillo Sitte, a Viennese architect writing in the 1890s, argued that the main ornaments of a city are its streets and squares (Sitte, 1901). Others would no doubt, add to Sitte's list of city ornaments and include, for example, parks, waterways and its main civic buildings. Even within his apparently limited palette Sitte was deeply concerned with the embellishment of streets and squares. He made an exhaustive analysis of the location of sculpture and fountains in urban spaces. He was equally concerned with the badly sited public building which, in his view, debased the urban scene. The great piece of sculpture or elaborate fountain are not the only features that decorate the city streets and squares. More mundanely, but of great importance for the quality of the urban scene, are items of street furniture such as telephone boxes, railings, signs and seats, or soft landscape features such as trees and shrubs. Adshead writing in 1911 made this important point about the furnishing of the street: 'We must bear in mind that all objects in the street - utilitarian or otherwise - are things to be seen - parts of an organic whole, each having their respective part and place. Olympus, Athens and Rome were each crowded with such objects, arranged for the most part in picturesque association' (Adshead, 1911a).

DECORATION FOR VISUAL PLEASURE

The most obvious, and perhaps the most important, dimension of decoration is its contribution to formal qualities, such as visual order or unity, proportion, scale, contrast, balance and rhythm. Ornament and decoration also have the capacity to unleash feelings, trigger reactions, feed the memory and stimulate the imagination. Decoration at one level is an activity giving visual pleasure, a formal physical process for visual delight; an activity for its own sake requiring no outside or higher authority to justify its existence.

Attitudes to the embellishment of cities with ornament and decoration range from a puritanical iconoclasm which sees such embellishment as decadent and pernicious, to one of joyous pleasure in the experience of complex, intricate and extravagant patterning. The Modern Movement (or movements) in architecture, epitomized by the writings of Le Corbusier, the pronouncements of CIAM, the work of the Bauhaus together with the much criticized post-Second World War city developments in Europe, collectively reflect a time when ornament and decoration in architecture was eschewed. In Britain, the Modern Movement in architecture can be seen as a reaction to the over-elaborate, and some would say debased, work of the nineteenth-century architects and their twentieth-century followers. Pugin writing in the mid-nineteenth century attacked much that he saw as vulgar in works of his own day, describing them as 'those inexhaustible mines of bad taste' (Pugin, 1841b). There may be a need for periods of puritanical zeal to rid city architecture of self-indulgent excess in decorative effects. Such periods allow time to reassess the value and role of decoration and ornament in the city.

This book, therefore, rejects the notion that there is something inherently immoral in decoration. Furthermore, it affirms with Scruton (1979) that there is no place in aesthetic debate for the 'moral argument'. Decoration and ornament on buildings is properly enjoyed for its own sake whether it is the intricate black and white patterns of the half timbered village, such as Weobley, or the traceried cast-iron arcades of Lord Street, Southport. A saturation of complex decoration stimulates primitive pleasure in the viewer. This book seeks to bring order where possible to this primitive activity. It is argued that from the theoretical and philosophical perspective so established it is possible to appreciate more fully the aesthetic experience of city ornament, supplementing with thought and judgement the undoubted sensuous and immediate pleasure of visual complexity. Such appreciation may then provide the basis for the organized use of ornament and decoration in future developments.

The aesthetic experience and visual appeal of decoration depends upon four factors. The first is the quality of the space which is both the setting for the decoration and which in turn is enhanced by it. The second is the physical form and the pattern of the decoration. The third is the circumstances under which the decoration is seen; for instance, weather conditions, particularly the quality of the light. The fourth factor relates to the perceptual framework of the observer, his or her mood, how he or she sees and what has been seen before.

PHYSICAL VARIABLES OF DECORATION

UNITY

While a full discussion of basic design concepts and their relationship to urban design has appeared elsewhere (Moughtin, 1992), it is proposed in this text to relate them directly to ornament and decoration. Probably the most important quality of any work of art is the clear expression of a single idea: any idea in any medium must, *a priori*, be complete, it cannot be composed of scattered elements without relation to each other. Urban design aims therefore to express complete unity in its compositions. Theorists such as Lynch, Alexander and Norberg-Schulz have tried to come to terms with the complexity of the concept of unity when applied to the field of urban design (Lynch, 1960; Alexander *et al.* 1987, Norberg-Schulz, 1980). For such writers, the study of human perception is important for the understanding of unity. The Gestalt school of psychology stresses the simplicity of visible form in the geometrical sense for producing clarity and singularity to distinguish figure from background. (Katz, 1950). Man, in order to orientate in the city, of necessity reduces the environment to an understandable simple pattern of signs and clues. In the words of Norberg-Schulz (1971): 'If we want to interpret these basic results of perception psychology in more general terms, we may say that the elementary organizational schemata consist of

the establishment of *centres* or places (proximity), *directions* or paths (continuity) and *areas* or domains (enclosure)'. Composition in urban design is the art, first of all, of creating visual unity out of a diversity of elements. For this purpose, a common theme for decoration is important to reinforce the normal tendency to see, understand and respond to vivid and coherent images. Secondly, it is to bring together these lesser unities into a city or town structure which itself is a visual and organizational unity. The goal of urban design has been given by Lynch as the development of a strong urban image. The structure of a pattern of decorative treatment with related themes emphasizing Lynch's five components is important for making the city whole in Alexander's (1987) terms and more imageable in Lynch's terminology (1960).

PROPORTION

An important characteristic of unity is the proportion of the parts or elements which make up a composition. Proportion is the method by which visual order is established, giving due weight to the compositional elements. For example, as Wölfflin (1964) points out: 'The Renaissance took delight in a system of greater and lesser parts, in which the small prepared one for the large by prefiguring the form of the whole'. Following the laws of proportion, some central idea, a visual element or group of related elements should dominate the whole composition. In urban design the 'dominant' may be the main town square around which the main civic buildings are arranged. Equally important for unity is the dominance of one decorative theme: the repetition of roof materials, pitch, skyline, ridge, verge and eaves details; the consistent use of floorscape materials and patterning; and the choice of street fittings of compatible form (Figure 1.2). The designer's task is to unify floor, walls and fittings in urban spaces which meet functional and symbolic requirements so that they are pleasing and attractive. The visual understanding of the city improves when the main structural elements are emphasized

Figure 1.2 Chipping Campden

using ornament and decoration. It is argued here that visual pleasure is related to this understanding of city structure.

SCALE

Scale depends upon the comparison of one set of dimensions with another set. Urban design is concerned with human scale, that is, the relationship of buildings and urban space to the size of a human being. Man is therefore the measure used for the built environment. The visual qualities of urban space and its architectural envelope and the act of healing or making whole the city are both closely related to the correct scaling of the urban landscape. Decoration and ornament play an important part in creating human scale in an area.

Taking man as the measure of scale, then for scale to be determined man must be visible. The mathematics for the measurement of scale has its origins in the work of Maertens (1884). Maertens found that we cannot distinguish any object at a distance more than 3500 times its smallest dimension. The limitations set by optical geometry define the varieties of urban scale. The nasal bone, according to Maertens, is a critical feature for the recognition of the individual. It is possible to distinguish individuals at about 12 m (40 ft) recognizing facial expressions; at about 22.5 m (75 ft) a person can still be recognized but at about 35 m (115 ft) the face becomes featureless while at 135 metres (445 ft) body gestures only can still be discerned. Finally it is possible to see people and recognize them as such from up to about 1200 metres (4000 ft).

The perception of the unity or wholeness of a building according to the theory developed by classical writers assumed a static viewer who at a glance could take in the whole composition of the façade. This condition is achieved when the viewer is at a distance from the building of about twice its height. At this distance a line from the building to the viewer makes an angle of 27° with a horizontal floor plane. According to Blumenfeld (1953), who followed this line of reasoning, the height of a building should be 9 m (30 ft) if it is being seen at a distance of 22 m (72 ft). For more intimate conditions where recognition of one's neighbours' facial expressions is useful, then the horizontal distance is 12 m (40 ft) and the building height is two storeys. A street width of 21-24 m (70-80 ft) for three storey façades and a street width of 12 m (40 ft) for two storey buildings, appear to coincide with the dictates of this commonsense definition of intimate human scale. At these scales and distances particularly on the ground and first floors, architectural ornament should have no decorative element with its smaller dimension less than 1-1.5 cm. Beyond the third floor, a bolder treatment of ornament is necessary for it to impinge upon the senses. A wide overhanging cornice, or highly modelled roofline is most effective at this viewing distance. At the extremes of human scale, sometimes referred to as monumental human scale, that is, at distances up to one mile, it is the roofline of the settlement which is appreciated and which can have a highly decorative profile.

It can be argued that a building is not appreciated only from some fixed point. There are many vantage points from which a building can be seen. This is even more apparent in the case of a city. The urban scene is presented to the viewer as a series of ever changing pictures in serial vision. In addition the length of time a particular view is seen can vary from location to location. Since, for example, a surface can be seen from a number of vantage points its decoration may have many layers, fine work for close inspection, ordering or

structuring elements for medium distances and bold shapes in silhouette for distant views. In western architecture there are two broad approaches to the ordering of architectural elements. The Classical school of design is the first of these approaches. It is derived from the theories of the Greek designers as interpreted by Vitruvius and his Renaissance followers. The second is derived from the master builders of the Middle Ages. The great works of Gothic architecture are made up of elements which are normally of constant size in relation to man and are absolute in regard to the building as a whole. The scale of the Classical order is relative to the entire building: columns, entablature and mouldings expand and shrink with the height of the building. The parts of the building are related to the size of the column base, therefore the scale of the building is absolute in regard to man. In the Classical building the number of elements such as columns, entablature and doors remain constant, their size varies; the elements in a medieval building remain constant in size but their number varies.

The two approaches to scale, while starting from different premises, have much in common and each can result in harmonious compositions. In the great buildings of the Classical and Gothic schools the concept of scale characteristic of the other method was not entirely rejected. The Gothic cathedral like the classical Greek temple front has a clear module of structural members and its western façade can be seen as a whole with clearly articulated elements. It has been suggested (Morgan, 1961) that the regulation found in medieval architecture owes something to the use of the mason's square for setting out building dimensions which ensured the 'recurrence of similar relations' infusing the whole design with 'some harmony' in all its parts. The temples of classical Greece never lost touch with human scale. Temples did not exceed 20 m (65 ft) in height and could be seen as a whole from the close viewing distance of 21-24 m (70-80 ft). The module was related to normal human size by its details being related directly to parts of the body; the fluting on

1.3

1.4

the column, for example, is the width of the arm. This system of modular design can and did lead to gigantism both in ancient Rome and in baroque buildings. It can also lead to confusion when two buildings using a different module are placed adjacent to each other. If, however, the module and overall building size are both conditioned by a viewing distance of 21-24 m (70-80 ft) then the building naturally takes on a human scale in addition to being harmoniously proportioned (Maertens, 1884).

This difference in proportional systems and attitudes to the scaling of buildings in European cities has led to the development of two main systems of ornamentation, the classical and medieval or gothic. Each has its typical decorative features and patterning. The result is not quite so distinct as the discussion so far would suggest: the distinction between the two approaches is blurred by a rich panoply of styles which appear more as a continuum rather than a simple dichotomy. Thus the urban designer must be aware of the subtleties when working within the older parts of the traditional city (Figures 1.3 and 1.4).

HARMONY

The theory of harmony in architecture is largely derived from the classical writers of the Renaissance: 'the aim of Classical architecture has always been to achieve a demonstrable harmony or parts. Such harmony has been thought to reside in the buildings of antiquity and to be to a great extent "built in" to the principal antique elements - especially to the "five orders"' (Summerson, 1963). The module or measure used to achieve harmony through proportion was the radius of the column at its base which was divided into thirty parts. All

Figure 1.3 Southwell Minster, Southwell
Figure 1.4 Palazzo del Museo Capitalino, Piazza Campidoglio, Rome

elements of the structure were multiples of this module. The five orders of architecture each had their own system of proportion, for example, in the Tuscan order the column height was fourteen modules, in the Ionic and Corinthian it was nineteen and in the Composite twenty (Summerson, 1963). All other parts of the orders varied in a similar manner. The purpose of such proportions is to establish harmony throughout the building. The harmony is appreciated through the use of one or more of the orders as dominant components of the building, or more simply by the use of dimensions repeating simple ratios: 'It is the property and business of the design to appoint to the edifice and all its parts their proper places, determinate number, just proportion and beautiful order; so that the whole form of the structure be proportionable' (Alberti, *Book I*, 1955). Alberti, writing about proportion, also states: 'Variety is without dispute a very great beauty in everything, when it joins and brings together, in regular manner, things different, but proportionable to each other; but it is rather shocking, if they are unsuitable and incoherent. For as in music, when the bass answers the treble, and the tenor agrees with both, there arises from that variety of sounds a harmonious and wonderful union of proportions which delights and enchants the senses' (Alberti, 1955). Beauty, according to Alberti and other Renaissance theorists, is a harmony inherent in the building imbued with a system of proportion which does not result from personal whim but from objective reasoning.

Searching for a secret mathematical harmony behind every form of architectural beauty is not confined to the Renaissance. According to Scruton (1979) this has been the most popular conception of architecture from the Egyptians to Le Corbusier. The fundamental concept is simple. Certain shapes and their arrangement seem harmonious and pleasing, others appear disproportionate, unstable and unsatisfactory. There is a general conviction that harmony in architecture results only if the shapes of rooms, windows, doors and, indeed, all elements in a building conform to certain ratios which relate continuously to all other ratios.

It is debatable whether such rational systems of proportion do produce the effects which the eye and mind consciously see and understand. The chapters which follow adopt Summerson's pragmatic attitude to proportion. He reduces the whole argument to a commonsense and practical viewpoint: 'To what extent rational systems of this kind do produce effects which eye and mind can consciously apprehend I am extremely doubtful. I have a feeling that the real point of such systems is simply that their users (who are mostly their authors) need them: there are types of extremely fertile, inventive minds which need the tough inexorable discipline of such systems to correct and at the same time stimulate invention' (Summerson, 1963).

The city must be experienced to be appreciated. Ornament and decoration, apart from distant silhouette, is best appreciated at close quarters. The city, however, is not simply an artefact to be viewed: the viewer is part of the city. The city is not only a visual experience, it is experienced by all the senses. Sounds, smells and texture are important: the cool sound of fountain spray or sonorous distant bell, the smell of garlic, hot chocolate and gauloise cigarettes on Parisienne streets, the rising heat from sunny pavements, or chilly dark shadows in distant alleyways. The measure for these experiences is the footstep. Distances are measured in paces. The pedestrian, therefore, is the module that gives proportion to the city. The rhythm of the pace is regulated by the floor pattern, it is quickened, slowed or brought to a standstill by the promptings of decorated pavements.

BALANCE AND SYMMETRY

There are other concepts such as symmetry, balance, rhythm and contour which have been used to analyse 'good' architectural design. These concepts, along with others that formed part of the earlier discussion, overlap and are mutually reinforcing: individual concepts do not, nor cannot, stand alone. There are two common sayings in the English language – 'a sense of proportion' and a 'balanced outlook' – both of which, when used about someone conveys the impression of a reasonable and well adjusted human being. Similarly a building which achieves balance is visually well adjusted, exhibiting a reasonable distribution of its component parts.

A simple pair of scales is often used as an analogue for balance in design. In the case of the simple scale, the force of gravity ensures that equal weights placed at equal distances from the fulcrum will balance. This idea of physical balance is extrapolated to the world of visual forms and is important in architecture both structurally and visually An obvious imbalance looks awkward, top-heavy, lopsided or even drunk. Symmetry, in its modern usage, has come to mean the balance of formal axial buildings. Symmetry of this type implies an axis of movement. Most creatures or man made objects which move directionally are symmetrical with regard to an axis of movement, whether they be flies, birds, mammals, aeroplanes or ships. Symmetrical arrangements in architecture, together with other man-made structures use this analogy of movement from nature. Consequently the symmetrical building composition is best appreciated while the viewer is moving along its central axis. Formal symmetrical decoration is also often best viewed from the central axis.

Asymmetry is the informal balance of non-axial components. It corresponds to the human figure in profile, which is capable of balanced positions of great complexity compared with the more static frontal symmetry. In simple terms a great weight close to the fulcrum of a balance will be balanced by a lesser weight at a greater distance. Similarly, the notional weights of architectural masses can also achieve a complex balance (Figure 1.5). There are no limits to the number of elements which form a unified composition providing they resolve themselves round a point of balance or a dominant

Figure 1.5 Church of San Francisco, Assisi

focal point of interest. It is to this point that the eye is first attracted, and to which it returns after an examination of the rest of the composition. Symmetrically balanced decorative patterning is usually associated with classical design and asymmetrical balance with medieval or Gothic compositions. Admittedly this is a great oversimplification; for example, Mannerism and Baroque compositions while employing many of the stylistic details of classical decoration achieve a movement in composition more closely associated with the work of medieval builders, sculptors and decorators.

RHYTHM

Rhythm is a basic characteristic of our nature. Children in the dark, listening to the tick-tock of the clock magically turn the sounds into a rhythmic beat, a pattern imposed by the mind. The great dancer moves rhythmically to the music both controlling and controlled by the motion, carried along by the experience. The ritualistic dances of

Figure 1.6 Palazzo Communale, Piazza del Campo, Siena

single column is just, well a point on a plan; or rather, a very small circle on a plan - it gives you the module of an order but nothing more. But two columns give you at once an inter-columnation, a rhythm, and there with the module, you have the germ of the whole building.'

CONTRAST

The triumph of unity over chaos, or the victory of order, is the condition of aesthetic success both in architecture and urban design. Good design, however, should avoid monotony and, therefore, it should have interest and accent. Some of the great pleasures in life derive from the contrasts found in nature. In architecture, much of the pleasure derives from similar contrasts. Entering the bright amphitheatre of the Piazza del Campo, Siena, from dark cavernous streets incised in the urban fabric is a stimulating urban experience; the contrast of horizontals and verticals in the Palazzo Communale confronts the visitor with further delight (Figure 1.6). If such contrasts were eliminated our lives would lose much intensity and vitality. Generally contrasts have to be kept within proportion to avoid perceptual overload. The correct balance between complexity and repose in architecture is the key to order. The same principle applies in the field of city decoration, as Smith (1987) points out 'Aesthetic success is conditional upon the victory of order, but there has to be sufficient complexity to make the victory worthwhile'.

Contrast in architecture, urban design and ornamentation is applied over an almost limitless field. There is contrast, of form and antiform, that is, of building and space, of street and square, soft and hard landscape, or colour and texture. In buildings there can be contrast in form, such as the sphere and the cube, the dome and the spire. In decorative details there is contrast of line or the contrast of objects in silhouette, contrast in direction, vertically and horizontally, or in colour and texture. Whatever the forms of contrast used, the main lines of the building or townscape should

Africa are imbued with heightened energy and the whirling-dervish dance transports participants to another plane. Rhythm in architecture has similar properties. It can be explained by reasoned analysis; but its stimulating and poetic effect transcends reflection. In the last resort rhythm in architecture and urban design is experiential.

Rhythm in architecture is the product of the grouping of elements; of emphasis, interval, accent and direction. It is the sense of movement achieved by the articulation of the members making up the composition. As Summerson (1963) explains: 'A produce a unified effect. A difficulty facing the designer lies in seeking the right degree of contrast. Taken to extremes such contrast can only produce discord. This occurs when the proportions of contrasting elements are so individually insistent that they compete rather than act as a foil to each other. The calculation of the right amount of contrast in harmonic composition for decoration and ornament as it is for any other aspect of design is a question of intuition and feeling. The rule of thumb, however, would seem to indicate the need for a clear dominant theme with contrasts of a compatible order. Extreme contrasts may produce disorder and lack of clarity.

CONCLUSION

The concepts discussed above have been used and can be used to analyse the aesthetic qualities of urban form. They are not, nor do they pretend to be, exact measures of quality. Some would argue that such measures are inappropriate. Nevertheless they provide a foundation for discussing the use of decoration and ornament in cities.

CLIMATIC BACKCLOTH FOR ORNAMENT AND DECORATION

The circumstances under which decoration is seen are important for its appreciation: indeed climatic conditions can affect the form of decoration. The clear bright skies of Greece may have stimulated the development of the crisply chiselled outlines of classical Greek architecture: the most subtle of profiles and the most complex mouldings can be seen and appreciated in the fine light (Figure 1.7). The building material, marble, was readily available for the perfect execution of such work. The stained glass windows of the Gothic Cathedral make the most of every shaft of precious sunlight infusing the building with colour and light, a contrast with the grey exteriors. The irregular and highly sculptural roofline of many medieval northern European cities

makes a dramatic statement against grey or watery skies. A bold overstatement is necessary in such circumstances. Roofscapes comprising buildings with subtle outlines of classical Greek origin appear bland and have little visual impact when seen in the light of the long northern European winter. Climatic conditions do not on their own offer a sufficient explanation for decorative style and form in architecture. Climate, particularly lighting conditions is, however, one parameter for the study of decoration in the city.

Figure 1.7 Temple of Athena Nike, Athens

PERCEPTION

Human beings attach meanings, values and objectives to their actions. We each have our own perceptual world developed within the boundaries of the social group to which we belong and with whose members certain aspects of the perceptual frame of reference is shared. The pensioner, the young parent, the business person, each has his or her own way of seeing, understanding and reacting to cues presented by the environment. It is those aspects of the perceptual worlds shared or held in common by groups which are of interest to the urban designer.

The communities inhabiting towns and cities are complex heterogeneous groups made up of diverse subcultures with differing values and aspirations. The understanding of an alien culture or subculture poses great difficulties. In our understanding of the world around us, we all start from our own cultural framework modified by a personal frame of reference. Such an analytical framework is deeply embedded in culture, and while it is necessary for structuring thought it can, in the process, limit understanding. Culture can be viewed as a filter, acting between the outside environment and the receiver.

While 'perceptual worlds' may differ, the process of perception and the formulation of a frame of reference are common. The stimuli which affect the senses of sight, hearing, touch, taste and smell are only a part of the energy emitted by the environment. There are limits to the ability of our senses to acquire information. For example, noises which are too high or too low in pitch are beyond the *threshold* of hearing. These thresholds can, however, change with experience: we filter background noise in a library so that we can work, or we do not notice the ticking of the clock. Our senses respond not simply to energy but to changes in energy levels. Once stimuli become familiar or non-threatening they stop being sensed. In the visual world we can become overloaded with stimuli in which case the senses cannot cope when editing or *perceptual selectivity* takes place. Information not required is filtered out. When this happens the attention as a general rule is drawn to stimuli that are:

> *large* rather than *small*
> *bright* rather than *dull*
> *loud* rather than *quiet*
> *strong* rather than *weak*
> *standing out from the surroundings* rather than
> *merged with their surroundings*
> *moving* rather than *stationary*
> *repeated (but not repetitive)* rather than *one off*
> (Buchanan and Huczynski, 1985)

Designers of advertisements, window display and road signs use this knowledge to attract and hold people's attention. They are important criteria for the urban designer in the consideration of decoration and ornament.

While the large will normally attract more attention than the small, the bright more than the dull, this general rule is frequently broken because these features or qualities do not appear on their own. A given stimulus will possess a *pattern* of features and it is to this pattern that our sensory faculties respond. The way these patterns are perceived also depends on the context. The setting for a precious stone is important for the full appreciation of the gem. So too the setting for a fine sculpture affects the way in which it is perceived. If set against a background of confusing shapes, colours and textures, even the greatest sculpture or fountain would be diminished: by contrast, however, a prestigious site adds importance and significance to the work.

Most of our perceiving can be described as categorization or classification. Classification systems for perception are complex. Objects may be classified as buildings, cars, etc. but those classifications are further refined so that buildings are further organized and structured in a number of different ways - by height, by use or by style for example. These categories or classifications are called *concepts*. The mental image formed for each concept enables the recognition of similar objects and their allocation within the individual's perceptual world. It is the image of the city which is of interest to the study of urban design; this text being particularly concerned with the strengthening of that image through ornament and decoration.

The retina of the human eye receives light on a two dimensional surface but we do not see simple mosaics of light and colour. For those with normal vision the world we see is organized into a three dimensional place. Incoming stimuli are organized and patterned in systematic and meaningful ways. There are a number of operations by which perceptual organization works. The eye, for example, tends to group together or classify stimuli that are physically close to each other, an operation called the *proximity principle* (Figure 1.8). The eye also tends to group together or classify stimuli that are similar to each other, an operation called the *similarity principle* (Figure 1.9). It is both of these tendencies which form the foundation of rhythm so apparent in the art of decoration.

There have been many experiments carried out to investigate the perceptual process of adults. It has been found that viewers are initially conscious that there is an object, something that stands out from and is different from the general background of the field of view. Next the object begins to assume a shape; first the outline is perceived, then the main interior features, then the colour and brightness. Then begins the process of classification and identification. There is a general tendency to perceive any shape with the maximum of simplicity, regularity and symmetry. If an observer is shown a shape which is almost circular, but slightly elliptical, he or she will categorize it and think of it as a circle. If shown an object which is slightly asymmetrical, the lack of symmetry will be overlooked and the shape simplified in the mind (Koffka, 1935). Gaps in incomplete or ambiguous patterns of stimuli are filled in ways which make them meaningful. This is called the *closure principle*: that is, we 'close' partial and confusing information to make it both intelligible and useful.

The forms perceived are in part determined by the actual physical shapes of objects in the field of view. There is, however, a tendency to modify the formal qualities of what is perceived, particularly if the information received is meaningless, that is,

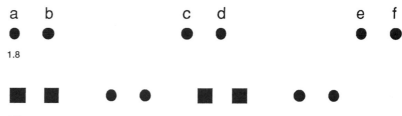

1.8

1.9

comprising forms which do not represent anything else. Such shapeless shapes tend to be perceived in as 'good' a form as possible; the 'good' form being striking, easy to perceive and remember. Qualities of 'goodness' in formal terms are simplicity, regularity, symmetry and continuity (Vernon, 1962). Decoration can be used to enhance the primary shapes in a design by emphasizing the outline of an object, so clarifying its form against the general background. The centre of an object can be emphasized with decoration, so intensifying the symmetry of the figure. Some great art clearly sets out to confuse and confound the eye by decomposing and eliding forms. It is suggested here, however, that the main objective of urban design, is to reinforce the understanding of the environment by strengthening the image of the city: the opportunities for confusing and confounding the observer using decorative, or any other techniques, in the field of urban design should be strictly limited.

The process of perception is responsible for selecting stimuli and arranging them into meaningful patterns. This process is influenced by the internal factors of learning, motivation and personality. These internal factors give rise to expectations making the individual ready to respond to some stimuli and not ready to respond to other stimuli. The framework of response to sets of stimuli is called the *perceptual set* (Buchanan and Huczynski, 1985). Each individual has a personal perceptual set and with it a personal and unique vision of what is out there in the environment. To some extent we have our own *perceptual world*. Different people can look at the same thing and perceive it in

Figure 1.8 Proximity principle
Figure 1.9 Similarity principle

different ways. It is futile to argue over the best interpretation. However, some groups within society share features of the perceptual sets and it is those shared perceptions which the urban designer tries to understand and which are addressed when attempting to decorate the city.

MEANING AND CONTENT

While the aesthetic qualities of decoration are to be respected, for a complete appreciation we must go beyond the visual appearance and examine meanings or content of city decoration and ornament. The inherent meaning of decoration can stand for the representation of place and/or the representation of the society occupying that place. In addition to symbolic meaning, decoration can impart information and enhance legibility.

The decoration of the city can act as a collective symbol, something that stands for a town and with which citizens identify. A notable example of such decoration is the annual bedecking of Blackpool with lights. To see 'the Blackpool lights' is an outing for young and old alike from neighbouring centres. Blackpool has become almost synonymous with the lights festival. This temporary embellishment follows the tradition of 'well dressing', an annual event in some small villages in rural Derbyshire. More permanent urban decoration epitomizing place can be found in Chester's intricate black and white half-timbered tracery; in the Art Nouveau street furniture of the Parisienne metro; in the Venetian Gothic lining that city's canals, or in the classical detailing of Bath's elegant eighteenth century streets (Figures 1.10 and 1.11). Decoration can, therefore, represent collective identity, signify place and make places distinct from one another: 'it testifies that a group of people share a place and a time, as well as operate in close proximity and with a good deal of interdependence' (Attoe, 1981). In this manner decoration contributes to the *genius loci*, while for Lynch (1960) it strengthens memorability.

Decoration can be read as reflections or indices of cultural processes and social values, as such it makes social meanings manifest. An examination of city decoration reveals how the city operates, which forces dominate life there and what the residents apparently value. Thus decoration is both a social symbol and evidence of social structure. For example, the decorative skyline of the city, in addition to standing for or symbolizing the society that occupies the city, can also provide information or clues about its organization and power structure. Thus decoration can be a social index representing the values of communal life. As an integral part of this index there are hierarchies of value and expression representing the scale of power, or 'pecking order' within the community. In some cases, there is an uneasy truce between powers which the embellishment of the city can proclaim. A delicate but decorative medieval church spire may compete with state power represented by a solid fortress or palace hung with flags and blazoned with coat of arms. At a different level, another important function is to offer individuals the opportunity to express themselves with more transient and often whimsical statements of personality, for example the personalization of the home with topiary work, or garden furniture of varying quality (see Figure 6.35).

In addition to the symbolic dimensions, decoration can also be utilitarian, an aid to orientation. Decorative skylines, for example, help individuals to know where they are and how to get where they want to go, as such the skyline has meaning as a landmark when it identifies localities in the city. Other decorative elements in the city serve this utilitarian purpose – the highly decorative street corner which acts as landmark; the growing intensity and complexity of floorscaping patterns that direct the foot along the path to journey's end; or the concentration of decorative work on the façade which indicates the entrance points. Those and other examples carry information necessary for efficient and effective movement within the public space of the city.

The classic study of orientation within the city is Kevin Lynch's, *The Image of the City* (1960). An important purpose, possibly the main purpose of ornamentation, is to make a city more memorable by giving identity and structure to its public realm. Decoration and ornament can be used to add coherence to each of Lynch's five components of city image. Embellishing these major components of individuals' mental images of the city enhances and strengthens the city's imageability. The image of the city, or the mental map carried round in the mind is the way in which people 'acquire, code, store, recall and decode information about their spatial environment - its elements' relative locations, distances, directions and overall structure' (Lynch, 1960). It is argued here that strengthening the image of the city for the citizen and visitor is the overriding purpose of decoration and ornament.

1.10

1.11

Figure 1.10 Gothic detailing, Venice
Figure 1.11 Georgian detailing, Bath

FUNCTION OF ORNAMENT AND DECORATION

The disciplined use of ornament and decoration begins with an understanding of its use and function on, for example, building façades; paved floorscapes or in the embellishment of civic space with fountains, trees or sculpture. While not adopting a high moral tone in the analysis of ornament, the authors nevertheless have great sympathy for the views of Alberti (1955) on this subject, in particular his dislike of 'everything that favours of luxury or profusion, and [I]am best pleased with those ornaments which arise principally from the ingenuity and beauty of the contrivance.' Although Pugin (1841) was taking sides in the 'battle of the styles' of the last century, his two great rules for design make sense to the twentieth century designer: 'first, that there should be no features about a building which are not necessary for convenience, construction, or propriety; second, that all ornament should consist of enrichment of the essential construction of the building . . . . In pure architecture the smallest detail should have a meaning or serve a purpose'. It is through analysis of the meaning, purpose and function of city ornament that discipline can be established in this important aspect of urban design.

The greatest pleasure from decoration and ornament in the urban realm will result when such embellishment is in harmony with its function. Ornament and decoration are not optional extras on a building or in a city: the city needs them as much as it needs a transportation network, car parks or city centre. Decoration and ornament share with all other facets of design the primary aim of creating unity. The aim of urban design, as Alexander (1987) maintains, is to create a series of properly formed wholes 'every part of a town, neighbourhood, a building, a garden, or a room, is whole, in the sense that it is both an integral entity in itself, and at the same time, joined to some other entities to form a larger whole.' Alexander goes on to define a 'whole' by saying 'A thing is whole only when it is itself entire and also joined to its outside to form a larger entity. But this can only happen when the boundary between the two is so thick, so fleshy, so ambiguous, that the two are not sharply separated, but can function either as separate entities or as one larger whole which has no minor cleavage in it.' Thus decoration and ornament in urban design can knit together buildings, streets, squares and neighbourhoods so that each, while remaining an entity, functions as part of a greater whole.

A subsidiary function of decoration is to ease the transition between the main design elements, between street and square, between structural elements such as floor and wall planes. It is also used to make the transition between the different materials used in the construction of the built environment. Examples include the decorative transition between column and lintel - the Doric capital being a perfect model, where the shaft of the column swells as if under pressure, straining with the load of the entablature. The profile of the capital, the echinus, prescribes a delicate curve, a perfect transition between two structural elements. The west front of the Gothic cathedral with its great pointed entrance repeats the shape of the door in a series of moulded arches offering the opening to the surrounding wall: the building elements of the wall and the door are welded into a unified whole using an ornamental device of great beauty (Figure 1.12). On a larger scale, the vertical wall of the street meets the ground plane with raised plinth, a pavement of patterned slabs, and raised kerbs, a slow transition from carriageway to vertical plain with the junction of the two repeated in a series of parallel lines. The decorated edging to footpaths within grassed or cobbled Oxbridge college courtyards is a delightful transition from material to material, an example of a decorated edge resulting from functional necessity.

An important role of ornamentation is to give emphasis to the most important part of a building, the most important buildings or the most important civic spaces. Elements emphasized in this way take on an added significance often imbued with symbolic meaning. The cathedral in the medieval or early Renaissance city was the building that received the greatest care and attention from the decorative artist. It was here that most time, effort and money was expended. The main civic building in these cities was important but it did not compete with the church which remained dominant in the life of the community. For example, the Palazzo Publico in Siena, a grand and imposing building, takes second place in significance to the intricately and richly decorated marble cathedral (Figure 1.13). More mundanely a change in external flooring or changes in level using steps are often employed to indicate change of

ownership offering a clear warning of greater privacy, while directional decorative paving and tree-lined routes emphasize important paths leading eye and foot to places or buildings of significance. Such devices may be as humble as the footpath or drive leading visitors to the main entrance or as grand as the great avenue of the Champs Elysée leading to the Arc de Triomphe and the tomb of the unknown soldier (Figure 1.14).

Decoration and ornament is an expensive business. It is therefore often confined to important elements – surrounds to doors or windows. Decoration is confined to the front of the building, the rear remaining plain (Figures 1.15 and 1.16). Other functions of decoration in the city relate more directly to functional necessity, such as

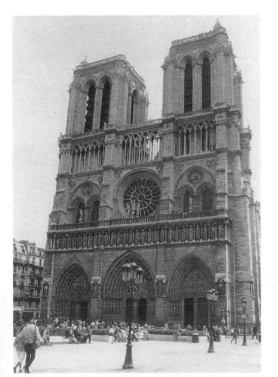

1.12

Figure 1.12 Notre Dame, Paris
Figure 1.13 Cathedral, Siena

1.13

1.14

1.15

1.16

Figure1.14 The Tuileries at one end of the Avenue de Champs Elysée
Figure 1.15 Decorated front, Regent Street, Nottingham
Figure 1.16 Undecorated back, Regent Street, Nottingham

providing shade, shelter, areas of safety, comfort or information. This category would include street planting, arcades, seating, lighting and signs. The elegant arcades of Bologna combine function - protection from the rain and the sun as well as channelling the pedestrians closer to shop windows - with street decoration (Figure 1.17). The rhythm and unity achieved by the colonnades are enriched by the decorations of the vaults, the detailing of the columns and the arches. Colour and figurines are used to enrich the environment and enhance the pleasure of shopping or prome-nading. Victorian shopping arcades in many British cities, notably in London, are examples of decorated shopping areas which provide a safe, protected and pleasurable shopping environment enriched with decorative masonry and wrought iron (Figures 1.18 and 1.19).

The design elements dealt with by the urbanist when analysing city ornamentation include the floor plane and enclosed walls of street and square together with the three dimensional objects placed within them. Of particular importance in the analy-sis of these elements is, for example, the junction of floor and wall plane; the roof line; street corners; changes in pavement level; ownership boundaries

1.17

1.18

Figure 1.17 Elegantly decorated soffit to street arcade, Bologna
Figure 1.18 Entrance to the Burlington Arcade, London

and openings in the wall plane. In a city designed for the pedestrian the floor plane is of major importance for this is the part of the environment that impinges most upon the eye. How often the amateur photographer produces a picture with a large, boring, unadorned foreground: this is the image which is produced on the retina. Like the façades along the road, the pavement should be carefully detailed to enhance the qualities of the street scene. The pavements of many continental streets together with the façades bounding them both define external spaces and decorate them to make the users experience a delight (Figure 1.20).

In a well-decorated city there are significant decorative changes as the eye moves from floor plane to façades and upwards to the skyline. For example, there may be smaller windows and elaborately decorated details on the ground floor, with the façade getting lighter with larger openings on the higher levels, and an articulated roofline completing the composition or conversely larger windows at basement ground level with upper floor windows becoming progressively smaller with the façade terminated by a simple cornice or balustrade. Where façades meet at street corners the junction is often treated with greater attention to decoration. The junction so formed becomes an important marker for orientation within the city.

PATRONAGE OF DECORATION

Richness and profusion of decoration is usually associated with the wealth and power of patronage. The use of ornament and decoration in the city, whether it is on the façade of buildings, the detailing of pavement, the munificence of park provision, the endowment of sculpture or fountains, can be seen as a display of power and the confirmation of status. At those times in the past when society, or more particularly a group in society, rejected decoration for ascetic or moral reasons, even its absence and the resulting iconoclastic or severe townscape is symbolic of the power of a group which is able to impose its puritanical will upon large sections of the community. For this reason city decoration must be examined in the light of prevailing social, economic and political conditions.

1.19

Figure 1.19 Interior, Burlington Arcade, London
Figure 1.20 Unity of pavement and façades, Tours

1.20

The legacy of the architecture and city design of some periods stands as testimony to the conscious exercise of power by some omnipotent, but now decayed, authority. This may not have been unchallenged power, for example, in many cities there was conflict between the autocratic and the mercantile elements, epitomized in their conflicting views of the city: one of grandeur or one of business. For example, Wren's grand plan for London was ultimately rejected by the merchants who wanted to rebuild their city quickly and get back to their businesses. Similarly John Nash was only able to proceed by displacing the poor (he was unable to displace the rich), and was effectively the forerunner of the even more high-handed railway companies of the mid-nineteenth century. In the middle of the same century there was Haussmann's destruction of the remains of medieval Paris. The attitude was that slums did not matter and that civic and national interests were more important than the local community. In a twentieth-century context, Adolf Hitler, in *Mein Kampf* (1971), lamented the disappearance of a tradition of monumental building in Germany, and in 1929 he promised that when the party took power 'out of our new ideology and our political will to power we will create stone documents'. It is not surprising that the Nazis' use of monumentality in architecture to advance their cause tainted, and continues to taint, this concept for the architectural profession.

In addition to changing technological, political and economic contexts which have limited or constrained the use of decoration, there has been and, to some extent still is, an ideological reluctance to engage in a monumental development of the city. The antipathy to monumentalism has also been accompanied by an equal abhorrence of decoration and city embellishment. This attitude of the orthodox Modern Movement in architecture was less concerned with the nature of traditional ornamental expression and more concerned with the need for a polemical stance that satisfied the political and social agenda of the early twentieth century and its implicit international, socialist and egalitarian viewpoint. Thus Modernists had concerns about ornamentation, and particularly about its commissioning, as a political and social expression of society. A problem for many in the Modern Movement was the inherent symbolism and legitimacy of monument and of monumentality, and thus of ornament and decoration. The question was who had the 'right' to decorate the city – individuals, autocratic rulers, autocratic landowners, Governments or developers? – and secondly how should it be decorated? Paradoxically, despite the reasons, origins and beneficiaries of many past monumental developments that have survived, such developments tend to be valued in today's democracies. How far Ceausescu's triumphal architecture in Bucharest will be appreciated by future generations, however, is difficult to predict.

An opposing view held by some revisionists of Modernism and advocates of some strands of Postmodernism hold that monumentality is made manifest by the architect who merely interprets the physical form of the city based on his or her knowledge of architectural history. One Post-modern critique of Modernism has sought to remove the concept of monumentality in architecture from its political and economic origin in order to justify, within our pluralistic and diverse contemporary society, the traditional manner of monumental expression (Krier, 1983). However, some would argue that monumentalism, when divorced in this way from its root causes, becomes little more than expensive pastiche. This reconstructed Post-modern attitude to monumentality is well expressed by Rob Krier. For Krier, monumentality is quite simply an inevitable fact of human settlement and civilization. Because of their mere existence, urban buildings obtain some significance in the public's perception of the city:

> Building is always about the occupation of a place. Architecture is about setting marks. In the free countryside we come across a tower. It directs our

way. Lighthouses, chimneys, steeples, city gates, defence towers, etc., belong to the archetypal symbols of uprightness. Towers symbolise the existence of human achievement, the triumph over earthly matters. Without doubt every tower has a monumental character as it rises above the environment. A monument is of course first and foremost a sign of power. Only the mighty potentate could afford to rise above his subjects by way of architectural manifestations. But he is mortal, whereas his monument will outlast him and will be celebrated by future generations as a cultural testimony. Without these 'signs of power' there would be no such thing as architecture: we would dwell in a desolate steppe (Krier, 1983).

What is perhaps most significant is the magnitude of the symbolism, it is usually at its most potent when freshly completed: over time, all other things being equal, it recedes into a state of relative benignness, becoming merely a physical artefact. The revisionist or postmodernists may argue that the symbolism can be stripped from the monument and the monument regarded simply as a physical artefact. However, the environment is less enriched if the monuments have no actual meaning. The physical effect may be true, but the functional aspect is false, theatrical and illusionary: superficial impact may not be enough, authenticity is also needed.

Since architecture is inevitably an expression of culture and more loosely of society and its milieu, there arises the question of which building types may today be rightfully treated as monuments and for whom or what deed should monuments be raised? The true and genuine function of monuments is as a symbol of religious, cultural or social significance and inspiration. For example, there have been statues to the leaders of the people, and to martyrs for the humanist causes of peace, justice, freedom and democracy. Monuments established as overt symbols or legitimizations of untrammelled economic, political or state power are irrelevant, dangerous and illegitimate in those states which purport to be democracies.

The glib statement 'We live in a pluralist society' is often used to justify the expansion of choice for those who can afford it and to limit access to goods and services for those already deprived of real choice. Certainly contemporary western society is pluralist: but what does that mean for the designer's attitude to decoration and ornament in the city? Arguably it means careful consideration of the needs of minority groups and the needs of the disadvantaged. Much work is now being undertaken into design to alleviate various problems, for example ensuring the safety of women in places characterized by male aggression towards women and also providing safe places for children's creative play and self-expression. Special textured paving can act as a cue for the blind and partially sighted, ramps for the disabled and other features important to minority groups offer the urban designer the opportunity to enrich the environment for all its users. There is an aesthetic dimension to the urban environment and designers should also think in terms of touch, sound and smell. Such a broadening of the definition of city decoration to include the smell of orange blossom, the sound of fountains or the cold touch of a marble bench while raising the prospect of a richer environment, nevertheless acts as an additional reminder of the duty to design for less able bodied members of the community.

An aspect of both architecture and urban design which is most subject to the whim of fashion is the form, content and distribution of ornament. This is particularly true at the moment. The pluralism of the postmodern period has witnessed an outburst of what became classified as architectural styles each with its own enthusiastic devotees. Styles may now co-exist in time and place or change in succession with bewildering speed. Clearly the present pluralism of style will remain for some time. The discipline of urban design may indeed be the factor which unifies otherwise disparate and often mutually incompatible architectural styles. Some form of ordered urban structure may yet emerge from a recognition of the primacy of context as the design criteria to be met in determining the choice of style and decorative treatment of new developments. It would therefore seem sensible to study city ornament and decoration in its historical context so that the knowledge gained will permit careful consideration in the choice of detail and street fixtures which blend with a particular townscape. Style by its very nature includes some features and excludes others: this is the essence of style, without exclusivity there is no style, without style there remains but fleeting fashion.

Much of this book is based on an analysis of past experience in the art of decorating cities. Historical examples will be used to derive, where possible, general principles. For the purpose of this book detailed historical analyses of individual cities has been rejected: peeling back the layers of history in an effort to understand the developing social, economic and political processes which account for a particular city form, while fundamental for the formulation of site specific proposals, generates little useful information on which to base a general theory of urban design. 'Peeling back the layers of history' is a vital step in the preparation of any proposal for specific intervention in urban structure: it is an essential part of method, important for the design process but not for general theory construction. This study aims to seek answers to the wider questions of how, why and where decoration should be used in the city. Answers to these questions, if indeed they are answers, can only be discovered from a wide ranging survey.

The main objective for this study of decoration and ornament in the city is to illustrate ways in which Lynch's concept of imageability can be strengthened by the judicious use of ornament. While establishing a mine of ideas for ornament and decoration, the historical survey does not itself examine the possibility that inhabitants of cities in former times perceived the city in Lynch's terms. This is a question not being asked of the evidence. In these studies nodes, paths and landmarks in past developments are identified from a later twentieth-

century perspective and in the expectation of enhancing a potentially powerful design tool for future use.

This study will concentrate upon the decorative treatment of areas in the city which are either wholly pedestrianized or where traffic has been calmed to such an extent that the pedestrian is in control of the environment. The images received from the environment for pedestrian and motorist are quite different. The motorist when travelling at speed receives but fleeting pictures from his or her surroundings. Considerations for the broad landscaping of motorways or their intricate geometry are for others working to different ends: here the emphasis is, very much, on how to please and stimulate the eye of the beholder walking at leisurely pace with time to stand and stare. For such an observer decoration and ornament take on great significance.

This book has eight chapters. This chapter has outlined the main philosophies and attitudes to decoration; the physical variables of decoration, its meaning, content and functions; ending with the social, economic and political framework for the subject. Chapter 2, develops a rational approach to the study of the use of decoration on wall surfaces in path and node. It illustrates the ways in which decoration on building façades results from functional or symbolic imperative. Chapter 3 analyses the types of corner in path and node and the variety of decoration used to emphasize external and internal junctions in street and square. Chapter 4 is a discussion of the city skyline roofscape and its decorative effect. It analyses the skyline and roofscape as both local and city wide landmarks. Chapter 5 analyses the design of the floor plane in path and node. The text will emphasize the reasons for decorative patterning which results from changes in paving materials. The chapter ends with a discussion of change of level in floor plane and soft landscaping. Chapter 6 entitled 'Landmarks, Sculpture and Furniture' discusses the design and location of three dimensional objects within the city. The chapter covers major landmarks such as important buildings or civic monuments and local landmarks which may be either ornamental or utilitarian. Chapter 7 begins with an outline of the theory of colour which is later related to townscape. Chapter 8, the concluding essay, is called 'The City of Today and Tomorrow: Ornament and Decoration'. Modern and Post-modern cities are contrasted. Some case studies of city decoration are outlined bringing together ideas discussed in the previous chapters and in particular to show how ornament and decoration can be used to emphasize the five components of city form distinguished by Lynch in order to ensure that each increment of development is a constructive attempt to decorate and unify the city by strengthening its image.

THE FAÇADE

2

INTRODUCTION

This chapter analyses the decorative use of ornament on the façade in street and squares. The façade is analysed in terms of formal, functional and symbolic qualities. For this analysis the façade is considered to comprise three main formal horizontal divisions - the base, podium or ground floor; the middle zone or main floors; and the roof or attic. Roofline and corner treatment will be discussed in Chapters 3 and 4. This chapter will, therefore, concentrate on the base of the façade and the main floors where the *piano nobile* is often located.

LOCATION OF ORNAMENT

Decoration on buildings and in the city generally is the means by which a variety of visual experiences are introduced to the viewer for his or her enjoyment. This quality is sometimes called richness (see Bentley *et al.*, 1985), but articulation is probably a more accurate description. The façade is an important element which presents this variety of experience to the viewer. People can choose different visual experiences from the fixed menu of the

urban environment either by changing their focus of attention in a given scene or by moving to another location and opening up a completely new vista or picture.

Visual monotony is a common feature of many urban environments dating from the post Second World War period. There has recently been a change in public attitudes to the built environment articulated in a vocal demand for a more decorative urban realm. The design professions wishing to satisfy this demand for ornamentation often copy past styles. While history is the source for many urban design concepts, thoughtless copying can lead to clumsy pastiche. It is important, therefore, to try to glean and evaluate the principles governing urban embellishment from a study of great works of the past.

Visual richness depends upon contrast; the contrast of elements such as window and wall; or the contrast of building materials, their colour, tone and texture; or finally the contrast of light and shade on the highly modelled surface. Visual richness also depends upon the number of elements in the viewer's field of vision. Too few elements despite a strong contrast gives little choice of objects at which to look. Here the composition

2.1

Figure 2.1 The Circus,
Bath
Figure 2.2 The Colosseum,
Rome

would look boring. When an elevation contains too
many identical visual elements they coalesce and
read as a single object with a tendency to also bore
the viewer. Five distinct elements appears to be the
lower limit where choice of object to view is sufficient to stimulate. A composition containing more
than nine elements may diminish in richness. A rich
elevation is one where from any given distance,
between five and nine elements are distinctly seen
(Bentley *et al.*, 1985).

The classical approach to decoration in its purest
form is based upon the 'orders of architecture'. The
façade being subdivided horizontally and vertically
by the main elements of the order, the entablature
and the column or pilaster. Each floor is emphasized
and distinguished by the use of a different order –
the external façade of the Colosseum, Rome, and
the Circus in Bath by John Wood being fairly typical
examples (Figures 2.1 and 2.2). Many fine buildings
from the nineteenth and early twentieth centuries,
however, use classical detailing for doors, windows
and other embellishments without following the full
rigours of the architectural orders. The less formal
decorative treatment associated with medieval
periods in Europe depends for its effect upon an all
encompassing pattern, a profusion of detail. In its
more ordered forms the decorative pattern follows
strictly upon structural imperatives. The internal
wall of the Cathedral nave expresses this idea to
perfection. The nave arcade supports the triforium
arches or blind storey which gives borrowed light
to the roof space above the aisle. Above the triforium is the clerestory which is the main source of
light for the nave. The decoration emphasizes the
elements in this structural pattern of superimposed
arcades subdivided into bays by massive pillars
which stretch from floor to vault where they branch
into elegant patterns of graceful arches to support
the weighty roof. A similar analysis of the external
façade of the Gothic Cathedral can also be made.
However, many fine buildings dating from the
nineteenth and early twentieth centuries use
medieval detailing for doors and windows in a

2.2

Figure 2.3 The Crescent, Bath

whimsical manner without following the structural discipline associated with high Gothic architecture. Both traditions of decoration, classical and informal, are the birthright of the urban designer in the late twentieth century. The recent rejection of ornament and decoration, requires a re-evaluation of these older and deeper traditions in order to establish a *modus operandi* for the designer of today.

A building may be said to consist of three main sections: a foundation or base that connects the building with the ground or pavement; a middle section with its rows of windows and possibly containing the *piano nobile*; and the roof zone which connects the building to the sky by silhouette. These three sections or zones of the building are common to both the classically and informally composed building. The relative weight given to each section in terms of decoration depends upon the position of the building in relation to the viewer, its height, mass and the location of its most important function. In the Crescent in Bath, John Wood the Younger expressed these three elements with great clarity. He combined the first and second

floors with one giant order. In this way he unified and differentiated the middle section of the Crescent both from the ground floor with its rhythm of doors and windows and also from the attic with balustrade and small dormer windows (Figure 2.3).

The emphasis of one or more of the major sections of the street façade provides an opportunity to introduce pattern, colour or highly modelled decoration. The elements may be emphasized by a simple horizontal string course or by a more distinctive treatment. The roofline will be dealt with in detail in a later chapter. The base connecting the building to the street pavement is probably the part of the façade most often noticed by the viewer (Figure 2.4). It is at this point, around the front door and parlour window that the residential street receives most attention to detail. A typical neo-classical residential street in London often has a white or cream rusticated stucco base which supports the main part of the elevation above usually in brick with stucco trim around the windows. The stucco base may extend below ground with a basement; the well being edged in fine black ornamental ironwork (Figure 2.5).

Figure 2.4 Perugia
Figure 2.5 Typical London house with main elevation in brick and stucco base

2.4

2.5

The most important zone for decoration in the shopping street is the ground floor. The shop front is the element of the façade which people have greatest contact with. The arcade is a most useful and highly decorative method of providing cover for the shopper in both the hot climate of southern Europe and in the wet and windy conditions of the north. The arcade also introduces a unifying element of continuity to the potentially diverse street scene made up of various retailers. With careful siting of bollards along the arcade, it also has the advantage that it discourages the 'ram raider' who, using stolen vehicles, drives into the shop window before removing its contents.

Shop fronts are a continuously changing feature of commercial streets as different retailers come and go wishing to place their distinctive mark upon the street. The shop front has three main horizontal divisions: the stall riser, the display window, and the fascia for advertising the retailer and his wares. The traditional shop front was a design based upon

functional needs and requirements. Windows were required to display the goods. The 1960s and 1970s witnessed a trend towards larger and larger windows so that the sales pitch could be made to those people passing in cars. As cities and central areas have been increasingly pedestrianized, with people passing by at a slower pace, shop windows have become smaller and more intimate again.

Below the shop window would be a stall riser. This would give protection from feet and dogs, and against rain splashing up from a dirty pavement. Ideally the stall riser is a continuation of the fabric of the building, so that the whole shop front integrates and harmonizes with the architecture. Many modern shop fronts have ignored this feature and have taken their shop windows right down to ground level. The floorscape of the recessed entrance also provides an often ignored opportunity for decoration. This flooring can either be a continuation of the flooring materials of the street or designed to harmonize with the design of the shop unit. Above the shop window would be the fascia carrying the details of the shopowner's name or activity. These have been the most controversial elements in the modern highstreet. Bland illuminated fascia signs of multiple and chain stores have weakened local and regional identity tending to make all highstreets appear similar. Traditional signs were either unilluminated or lit by external fittings which of themselves would be decorative. The fourth element of the shop front, the door, is a location for special decorative treatment. The decoration of the window surrounds should not distract from the merchandise and its display, nevertheless, some of the traditional shop windows dating from the last century are fine decorative settings for the display of goods for sale (Figure 2.6). They are good models on which to base a modern interpretation of shop front design, having more aesthetic appeal than the standard 'house style' store front with long fascia that proclaims ownership across an array of fine upper storeys.

The finer articulation of the middle zone of the façade consists in its relief. Elements such as cornices, string courses and vertical edging along property boundaries define the zone. Within the zone the articulation is largely achieved through the decoration around the edges of windows, niches, or the treatment of projecting bays, balconies and stairwells. Often the ornamental work is of contrasting colour and material from the main background walling material. One or other of the materials, background or decorative material, should be seen to clearly dominate the composition. There should be no hesitation, no indecision as to which is the main colour or material. Since the trim is the most

Figure 2.6 Renovated Victorian shop front, York

expensive part of the construction it is usually the smaller in expanse and often successful for that reason.

Other important considerations for the location of ornament are the distance of the viewer from the façade; the angle at which it is viewed; and the time the viewer has in which to look at the composition (Bentley *et al.*, 1985). A prime location for architectural decoration is at the external corners of buildings, particularly if the corner is at the junction of several streets. The external angle of the building will be dealt with in detail in a later chapter. However, it should be noted here that this

2.7

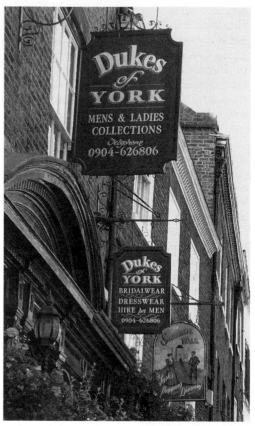

2.8

Figure 2.7 Haymarket Theatre terminating the vista from St James Square, London
Figure 2.8 Cantilevered signs, York

particular part of the street allows the viewer to approach the feature from many different angles and so to appreciate the embellishment fully. The closing wall of a street 'T' junction offers similar opportunities for decoration (Figure 2.7). The termination of the vista may take the form of a tower or a projecting bay.

The closer the viewer is to a building the greater the opportunity to see and appreciate intricate detailing. The bland flat elevation at close quarters is at its most boring. For those parts of the building seen at a distance of about twelve metres (40 ft), the first six metres (18 ft) of the building constitute the area seen most readily and are the place where detailed ornament should be concentrated. From this position of about twelve metres, areas of the façade above six metres become more difficult to see with comfort; the head has to be tilted considerably and a conscious effort made to appreciate detailing on a wall higher than about twelve metres or at an angle of forty-five degrees to the eye. From

distances greater than twenty-four metres (80 ft) larger areas of the façade can be seen as a pattern but decoration has to be bolder to be observed and features such as windows grouped to form more dominant objects in the field of view. Solving the problem of foreshortening in perspective, that is, the apparent loss of size in objects at greater distances from the eye, was well known to the Ancient Greek architect and sculptor. For them, it was common practice to increase in size the mouldings furthest from the eye. Those projections and details at heights above a three storey building, if they are to impinge strongly on the viewer's perception, need to be more robust than corresponding details at ground level. In narrow streets where the façade is rarely seen as a frontal elevation large overhanging string courses, highly modelled cornices, projecting bays, undulating wall surfaces, cantilevered signs, clocks and flower boxes are appropriate forms of street decoration (Figure 2.8).

THE STREET

Vitruvius in the first century AD described the street scenes used at that time as theatrical backdrops (Vitruvius, 1960). The general formal qualities of the scenes still retain a powerful image for the European urbanist. The three scenes according to Vitruvius are tragic, comic and satyric. Each street scene has a quite distinctive decorative effect. In the tragic scene, the street is 'delineated with columns, pediments and statues'. It is a formal classical street. The comic scene in contrast is the home of the ordinary man and is decorated with balconies, rows of windows and dwellings. Serlio (1982) in *The Five Books of Architecture*, published between 1537 and 1545, illustrated the scenes described much earlier by Vitruvius. The comic scene Serlio depicted as an informal arrangement of town houses, towers, chimneys, balconies and windows with pointed or round arches. It is a mixture of styles typical of many Victorian streets in Britain. The satyric street Vitruvius describes as being decorated with 'trees, caverns, mountains and other rusticated objects in a landscape style'. This description could fit many suburban developments in the garden city style. The three theatrical scenes of Vitruvian origin are still part of a living urban tradition and are vital concepts in the urban designers repertoire.

Streets constitute the most common parts of the city. Within the framework of generic street types outlined by Vitruvius there is great variety. Streets can vary in length, cross section, shape, character, function and meaning. In addition, streets may change some or all of these qualities over time. An appreciation of the street façade and its decoration is dependent upon an understanding of the street's development, context, role and function. Using case studies this section of the chapter aims to analyse the ornamentation of street façades in terms of these factors. It will also explore the role of decoration as a unifying theme in an urban realm of great complexity.

Urban streets can be broadly grouped into three functional types. First, there are the great civic streets dominated by civic buildings such as theatres, concert halls, museums and government offices. A particularly good example is Pennsylvania Avenue in Washington DC. Second, there are the commercial streets - the streets with which we most often identify our city. Regent Street, London, Boulevard Haussmann, Paris and Fifth Avenue, New York, fall within the category of commercial streets. Third, there is the residential street. Residential streets constitute the largest part of urban areas. They vary considerably in terms of their decorative quality ranging from the monotonous to the richly decorative.

There is no well-defined boundary between street types. As cities grow or decline, commercial streets may give way to residential functions or vice versa. In addition, at any given time streets may possess two or three of the main functions. However, a street may be classified according to its main characteristic and this is usually clearly distinguished.

CIVIC STREETS

The civic street lends itself to the decorative treatment associated with the Vitruvian tragic scene. Grand scale in civic streets is achieved using vertical elements. Columns, pediments and other classical elements are used to achieve a unity despite the

Figure 2.9 The Rajpath,
New Delhi

variety of different building types, heights and massing. In Pennsylvania Avenue, Washington DC, neo-classical façades of museums and government buildings juxtaposed with modern buildings define a highly decorated street of great complexity where unity is achieved through the use of materials and the repetition of small scale cues. On a civic street such as Pennsylvania Avenue, different buildings add to the richness by expressing externally their functions. The extension of the National Gallery by I.M. Pei is such a building adding to the street its own decorative effect. The height control in Washington limits the effectiveness of the roof line as a decorative element: the street under these conditions achieves its effect without the contribution of an exciting skyline.

The Rajpath in New Delhi is another example of the monumental civic street. It is unified by Lutyens' plan; the imposition of a classical style of architecture with a strong Moghul flavour; the repetitive use of red and yellow sandstone and the employment of a fine formal landscape treatment (Figure 2.9).

The Embankment in London lines the Thames. Established in the late nineteenth century, it reinforced the tradition established by the great aristocratic houses built between the Strand and the river in the seventeenth and eighteenth centuries. The result of this early development had been large plot sizes and the tradition of buildings with two façades, one addressing the road, the other the river. The buildings of the Embankment in the nineteenth century made the sweeping riverscape significant in a decorative sense. There is a regular massing of 'palaces' but each is different in detail, articulation and materials. The buildings use classical elements with a mainly vertical emphasis as the main decorative theme. This is a lively waterfront with an imposing presence and a decorative theme which is in keeping with the grand scale.

COMMERCIAL STREETS

Commercial streets because of their function, decorate the city: these are the streets where the quality of design achieved by decoration contributes to business prosperity. The life and movement of pedestrians on the pavement stimulated by the commercial activities, is itself a vital contribution to decorating the city. Commercial streets can take on the classical appearance of the Vitruvian tragic scene or the quaint medieval charm of the market town imbued with the character of the comic scene. Whichever form the commercial street takes it is the backcloth to the daily theatre of business life, the heartbeat of the city. Regent Street has decorated the central part of London for nearly two centuries. It has been, and still is, a major magnet for attracting high quality retail and ancillary services. The great pleasure that Regent Street gives the user and tourist lies in its graceful curves which, as one walks along it, present an ever changing and unfolding visual scene. However, a curving street was not John Nash's original intention (Summerson, 1935). He had envisaged a straight street linking the royal lands in the north to the important parts of London in the south, but was forced by the awkward patterns of property ownership in the intervening fashionable areas to resort to curves. Whatever its genesis, Regent Street is a spatial delight. Prior to the First World War that spatial delight would have been complemented by the architecture defining the space of the street. Alas Nash's Regent Street is now gone, lost in the insensitive redevelopment of the 1920s and 1930s when many leases fell due, and in the rebuilding after the bombing of the Second World War. The modern observer can only mentally reconstruct the experience of Nash's Regent Street. The ground plane of this street, for example, was a rich texture of granite setts in keeping with the scale of the street architecture of Nash and his contemporary designers.

Nash's Regent Street was a triumph of picturesque visual planning. Although Nash was

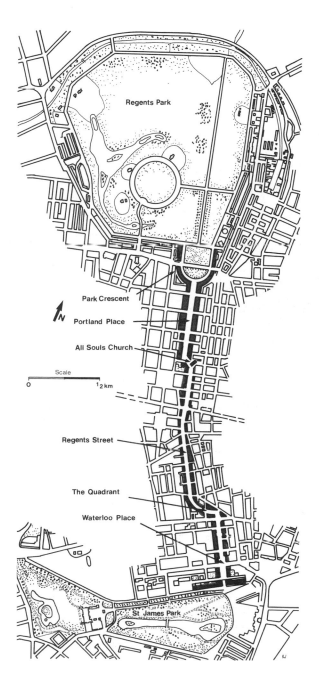

Figure 2.10 Plan of Regent Street, London

Regents Park

Park Crescent

Portland Place

All Souls Church

Scale

0   1 2 km

N

Regents Street

The Quadrant

Waterloo Place

St James Park

Figure 2.11 The Quadrant, Regent Street, London
Figure 2.12 Regent's Park Crescent, Regent Street, London

2.12

unable to design all of the building façades himself, as the entrepreneur putting the scheme together he was able to coordinate the various façade designs. The visual unity of the original Regent Street was ensured by the consistent use of a classical style and its execution in painted stucco, a building material often regarded as inferior to stone. Nash did, however, manage to design the critical façades that closed vistas and the important accents where the street changes direction. Bacon (1978) remarking on 'the sinuosity of Regent Street' suggests that the aesthetic quality of the street may be due to 'the superb handling of the changes in direction of the street by cylinders and flat domes of the bordering buildings'. It was at these points that Nash's skill as a decorator of the city becomes most apparent. The decorative detail and articulation of Regent Street occurred within the successive spatial episodes and, more particularly, at the junctions of those episodes so that no portion of the street was uninterrupted by square, circus or crescent for more than a few hundred metres. This decoration was rarely elaborate or complex, rather it was suitably restrained, subtly reinforcing the significant spatial qualities of the street (Figures 2.10 to 2.12).

As originally built, the processional route of Regent Street, at one end, began at Carlton House - the Prince Regent's residence. The vista southwards through Waterloo Place would originally have terminated at Carlton House demolished in 1827. The axis of Lower Regent Street now focuses on the York Column and an imposing flight of steps leading towards St James' Park, extending the route onto The Mall leading to Buckingham Palace. The initial vista northward through Waterloo Place and Piccadilly Circus was terminated by the apparently substantial presence of the County Fire Office. Even though the County Fire Office was not as substantial as it appeared, the scale of its elevation produced a convincing effect within Lower Regent Street. The junction of Lower Regent Street with Piccadilly formed the original Piccadilly Circus. To avoid the impression of crossing Piccadilly, Nash placed identical curved buildings on each corner to give each street equal significance. However, the spatial qualities of this circus were badly distorted when Shaftesbury Avenue was cut into the circus in 1886 and little trace of the original circus remains today. From the County Fire Office, Regent Street turns sharply through ninety degrees into the majestic sweep of The Quadrant. The decorative detail here again was restrained so that little detracted from the grace of the space. The use of covered colonnaded walkways down its whole length (removed in 1848) and a uniform architectural treatment established unity and grandeur.

As at Piccadilly Circus, Nash enhanced the crossing with Oxford Street with a circus to give each street equal significance. However, the circus as rebuilt between 1913 and 1928 is weakly-defined, its spatial qualities out of proportion with the scale of the streets forming the crossing. To the north of Oxford Street, Nash was obliged, for practical reasons, to change the direction of the street to pick up the line of the earlier Portland Place. In the hands of a lesser designer this could have resulted in an awkward link. Nash resolved the problem with masterly precision: All Souls' Church with its adroitly placed circular-spired vestibule was used both as a terminal feature at this awkward junction and as an element which neatly resolves the offset of the street. The siting of the circular drum shows a fine appreciation of urban form; the church becoming a decorative urban statement and a masterpiece of civic design. Further north, Regent Street incorporates Portland Place built by the Adam Brothers. Portland Place was considered in the early eighteenth century to be the finest street in London. The broader and stately proportions of Portland Place slow the visual pace of Regent Street. To the north of Portland Place, Regent's Park Crescent and Regent's Park Square function as a powerful connection between Portland Place and Regent's Park. The semi-circular sweep of the Ionic colonnaded crescent directs the movement both out of and into Portland Place. Its decorative detail being restrained

Figure 2.13 Arcaded Parisian street

and polite, the unadorned sweep of the space alone is sufficient, presenting a magnificent opening or coda to the street sequence.

Boulevard Haussmann, Paris, in function and in terms of its use of neo-classical elements is very similar to Regent Street. In Boulevard Haussmann major stores express their corporate identity while showing respect for the street by using materials, details, a style and scale which is in keeping with the surrounding street context (Figure 2.13). The ground level of the street accentuates horizontality with large glazed areas, facing and corners which both support and contrast with the verticality of the rest of the building façade. Colonnades and arcades are another way of decorating commercial areas. A typical example is Bologna. The central area is highly decorated by the extensive use of repetitive elements, rich detailing and the subtle use of colour (Figure 2.14).

It is, of course, possible to achieve highly decorated streets without using classical elements, as in the case of Amsterdam. The narrow frontages along the canals in Amsterdam have resulted in a

2.14

Figure 2.14 Piazza
Maggiore, Bologna
Figure 2.15 Canal scene,
Amsterdam

rich urban scene. The vertical emphasis of the architecture is a result of the medieval ownership pattern and taxation. The streets of narrow gabled fronts are reflected in the canals extending their apparent height and increasing the effect of verticality. The buildings show great respect for context: window shapes, details, materials, gable and colours blend to form a highly decorative and unified street scene (Figure 2.15). A similar form of gabled street elevation can be found in those areas of European cities where medieval sections of the city survive. A particularly good, though small, example is The Shambles in York (Figure 2.16). The ownership boundaries are narrow, the frontage vertical and the distance between street walls narrow, decreasing in width with each successive cantilevered floor. The small scale of the architecture and the sense of tight enclosure maximize the decorative effect of shop

2.15

2.16

2.17

Figure 2.16 The Shambles, York
Figure 2.17 Baroque façade, Vienna

window, signs, paving and half timbered structure. This is a charming street in which to shop, a decorative gem in York, a city of many fine streets.

RESIDENTIAL STREETS

London and Paris are cities which are well endowed with decorative and decorated streets. Streets in Belgravia, Mayfair and Sloane Square use both neo-classical and Georgian decorative features to achieve a human and distinctive environment. The same can be said of the streets of Paris, especially north of

the river in the Eighth Arrondissement. Stone and stucco are used throughout to create small unified areas of great identity in an environment of fine grain and rich texture.

Prague and some parts of Vienna in contrast have streets which are decorated with fine examples of Baroque and Art Nouveau façades. The rich ornament, curves and elliptical shapes decorate the Baroque street with profuse detailing and disturbing movement. Art Nouveau buildings contribute to ornament and movement in a similar fashion to their more ponderous neighbours but with lightness and less gravitas (Figures 2.17 and 2.18).

Figure 2.18 Art Nouveau façade, Prague
Figure 2.19 Villa by T. C. Hine, Park Estate, Nottingham

2.18

2.19

The decorated street is not confined to those occupied or built by the more affluent citizens. Britain has a wealth of nineteenth-century working class streets finely decorated with the ubiquitous bay window and with polychromatic patterned brickwork. Large parts of British cities are devoted to the suburban street where buildings and their landscape jointly create decorative complexity without, in the best examples, disarray. Although all suburbs are not of the quality of the Park Estate in Nottingham, it nevertheless exhibits many of the attributes associated with the suburban street.

The Park Estate is a unique housing area to the west of Nottingham city centre which was developed by the fifth Duke of Newcastle in the mid-nineteenth century. The fourth Duke had initiated the development of a residential estate in the parkland of the castle in 1827 but abandoned his

plans after rioters had burned the Castle in 1831 (Brand, 1992). Retrospectively this was fortuitous as the 1827 plan by Peter Fredrick Robinson proposed a contextually insensitive rectangular grid for the area, a crescent-shaped hillside running down from the Castle. A few houses had already been built on the crest of the hill in a Regency style which emphasized the windows by white stucco borders and the entrances by elaborate pilasters or columns. Although the edges of the Park Estate had been substantially built by 1856, the roads of the Park Estate were laid out according to Hine and Evan's 1861 plan (Gadbury, 1989). Hine (1814-99), a very restrained and accomplished architect, was influenced by John Nash. The road layout is centred on a pair of circuses - Lincoln Circus and Newcastle Circus. The axial roads leading out from the circuses cut the elliptical roads surrounding the circuses. The roads are not sufficiently well-defined spatially to be termed streets and their decorative qualities derive from the location along them of individually designed villas. This layout, combined with the rather steep terrain, was able to give a high degree of privacy to the moderately large villas designed for the emerging industrialists and professionals of Nottingham. The villas with large gardens were surrounded by high walls, often with quite elaborate detailing including coloured brick courses and shaped bricks for top courses. Inside the Park Estate most of the houses were brick with some stucco and a few Italianate buildings on the higher levels. Hine used brick with some Tudor elements - mainly in the upper levels - and turrets in corners to embellish his buildings. The lower levels of the houses were hidden behind garden walls and shrubs, it made sense, therefore, to decorate the upper levels where the rich ornament could be appreciated by the passer-by. Turrets and elaborate details made each house unique and expressed the wealth of its owner (Figures 2.19 and 2.20).

The houses of Nottingham's other leading Victorian architect, Watson Fothergill (1841-1928), are immediately recognizable by the elaborate Gothic details incorporated on the upper levels. Turrets are used to accentuate the massing and decorate the visual scene for pedestrians as well as expressing the wealth of the owners. Fothergill's designs for the Park Estate are more restrained than many of his designs elsewhere in Nottingham, but they still incorporate elaborate sculptured details around the windows and doors.

The decorative pleasure of the Park Estate derives from the diversity, contrast and juxtaposition of highly individualistic buildings, an environment created by the 'one-up-manship' of the middle classes. The contrast is suitably epitomized by the comparison of Hine's many broadly similar villas with the fewer, but more extravagant, villas designed by Watson Fothergill. What prevents the Park Estate from descending into visual chaos is the unifying effect achieved by the trees and planting,

2.20

Figure 2.20 Detail of doorway, Park Estate, Nottingham

the formality of the regular layout of villas on ample plots, the limited range of building materials (stone, brick, timber and tile) and the brief time span of the estate's development, which ensured the relative coherence of the area while also permitting a startling diversity. The end result is a visually rewarding collage held together by landscape.

MULTI-FUNCTION STREETS

Not all streets can be neatly categorized according to functional type. Some streets such as those of the Lace Market, Nottingham, have changed during the progress of time, while some such as the main street in Saltaire, Yorkshire were designed with many functions in mind. The main street in Saltaire is residential, contains the main commercial area of the town and also the main civic buildings. If

Figure 2.21 Remnant of
original paving, Saltaire
Figure 2.22 Lion and
railings, Saltaire

2.21

2.22

sustainable development remains an important goal in the future and if movement, and therefore energy efficiency is a priority consideration, then the multi-function street will be the norm. As such it will be streets like Victoria Street in Saltaire that will be the model for future urbanists.

Saltaire was established in 1851 when Titus Salt decided to move his business out of a growing and congested Bradford. Inspired by one of Disraeli's novels, *Sybil*, Titus Salt employed the architects Lockwood and Mawson to build his new town four miles from Bradford on the River Aire between the Leeds-Liverpool canal and the main railway line

from Scotland to the Midlands. Being outside Bradford, it was cheaper to build, not subject to the Borough's rates nor to its restrictions on building which would have prevented the more novel aspects of the scheme (Dewhurst, 1960).

The main street Victoria Road, is the spine of the development. The street has lost its original paving. Some idea of its texture and patterning can be seen in the remnants of paving in one or two small areas of other streets (Figure 2.21). The entrance to Saltaire is through a little square enclosed on one side by the hospital and on the other three sides by the almshouses. The almshouses are particularly ornate and beautifully detailed with Gothic revival ornament. Walking down Victoria Road is a delightful aesthetic experience. The spaces are architecturally modulated, buildings are arranged on either side of the route, in mutually reflecting projections or axially composed elevations. The whole street is an exercise in inflection, that is, the echo of feature with feature across the space, the 'minuet of street architecture' (Edwards, 1926). At the main square where the school faces the community hall are four reclining lions, purchased by Titus Salt when they were found to be too small for the original intention of decorating Trafalgar Square. It is here too, at this main accent of the street, that the finest ironwork is to be found (Figure 2.22).

Although the grid iron plan of Saltaire was similar to the one used for much of nineteenth-century working class housing, in Saltaire it did not plumb the depths of monotony found elsewhere (Moughtin, 1992). In part, this may be due to the small scale of the development but more probably because of the thought given to the architectural detailing. Salt had commissioned a social survey amongst his workers in order to determine the type and quantity of housing required for the town. According to Dewhurst this was the 'first time that it had occurred to anyone that a workman with ten children needed more rooms than a workman with one child' (Dewhurst, 1960). As a consequence, the variety in house type built into the programme gave the architects greater scope to articulate the long street elevations (Figure 2.23). Avoiding monotony is the first step in making a street pleasurable. Large houses were placed at ends of terraces or at strategic points where emphasis was required. The long street frontages stepping down the contours were also judiciously broken up with pavilions of larger houses which accommodated the change in roof line in an architecturally controlled manner.

The tall narrow spaces of Nottingham's Lace Market make it one of Britain's unique industrial cityscapes, containing some of the finest nineteenth century industrial architecture. Until the nineteenth

Figure 2.23 Street scene, Saltaire

century, it had been a residential area of large mansions and well laid-out gardens, but in the nineteenth century it became the world centre for the lace industry. The decorative qualities of the Lace Market establish it as an identifiable district, not by distinct boundaries or edges but by virtue of the intensity of its character. That character is derived directly from the nature of the activities that were housed in the buildings.

Stoney Street is one of the two principal streets of the Lace Market, with five and six storey warehouses built with the distinctive red-orange Nottingham brick. They stand squarely up to the edge of the pavement creating a street with a canyon-like effect. The narrow space of Stoney Street exhibits the principal decorative theme of the Lace Market: rhythmic arrays of solid and void in otherwise austere and functional façades: the warehouses and factories were utilitarian structures, requiring good lighting conditions for lace making. Thus the design of the façades, often of load-bearing masonry construction with large window areas, was a skilful engineering achievement. The façades range

2.24

2.25

from the stridently utilitarian to those that, while
remaining simple and functional, are beautifully
proportioned and detailed.

The austere façades are complemented and
counterpointed by the deliberately embellished
doorways and entrances. Industrialists wishing to
impress clients, customers and their fellow
merchants, concentrated decoration at ground level
and around entrances. The potential tension of the
interplay between these decorative themes is well-
illustrated in the Rogers and Black factory (1879) at
the corner of Warser Gate and Stoney Street, a
bizarre juxtaposition of an exuberant, but
awkwardly-scaled 'Renaissance' entrance portico and
a simple, restrained proto-modernist façade. At a
more detailed level there is a wealth of ornament
both as applied decoration and in the typically

Victorian treatment of windows and other details,
using standard mass-produced building components
with flair and imagination (Figures 2.24 and 2.25).

Like the Park Estate, Stoney Street features the
work of Nottingham's two most prominent architects: the restrained and disciplined T.C. Hine and
the more flamboyantly decorative Watson Fothergill.
T.C. Hine, the earlier of the architects, built one of
the first model factories in the Lace Market, the
Adams and Page building. The setback entrance and
the grand flight of steps lend the building an
impressive air of grandeur which relieves the claus-
trophobic effect of this part of the Lace Market. In
the entrance of this building can be seen a lattice-
work motif reminiscent of Nottingham Lace.

Within the Lace Market, Fothergill's decorative
talent can be seen in his factory for Cuckson,

Haseldine and Manderfield (1897) on the corner of Stoney Street and Barker Gate giving identity and character to the very heart of the Lace Market. Although relatively restrained by Fothergill's standards, as a piece of decoration the building provides counterpoint to the more austere and restrained buildings of the Lace Market by incorporating polychromatic brickwork, which is atypical of the Lace Market.

To the west and running almost parallel to Stoney Street is St Mary's Gate, the vertical scale of which is lower and less dramatic. At its northern end there is a large vacant site facing the rear elevation of T.C. Hine's Adams and Page building. This austere, but elegant building boasts decorative motifs, expensive ironwork and stone reliefs carved with subjects appropriate to the lace making industry. This elevation also shows the characteristic continuous attic or 'lantern' windows lighting the mending and inspection rooms. Just off St Mary's Gate is Pilcher Gate. On this street, stands another Fothergill building atypical of the Lace Market. Built for Samuel Bourne and Company in 1889, this warehouse, in contrast to Fothergill's other Lace Market building, is a simple and uncluttered statement: an essay in the decorative power of changing ratios and proportions of solid and void in brick, glass and stone.

THE SQUARE

Many of the principles of decoration so far discussed apply equally to the square or street. Only the main points of distinction will, therefore, be discussed in the following section. The square or piazza is a place of rest within the busy street network. In the terms of Lynch (1960) it is a node of activity, the junction of many paths: it is the centre or the portal of a district, town or city. As such the node is a place where people gather and rest before continuing the journey. The piazza, place or square, therefore, provides an opportunity for the urban designer to display the art of city decoration. At these points in the public realm the citizen is in an ideal location to appreciate the finer points of city embellishment.

Each city, according to Camillo Sitte (1901; Collins and Collins, 1986) has a number of squares but one square or group of related squares at its centre is the most important and is larger than the rest. It is here, according to Sitte, that the community displays to greatest effect its public art, great sculptures, fountains and obelisks. It is here too, that the important and most decorative buildings are located. Since Sitte was writing, cities have changed dramatically in size, scale and function, nevertheless, this principle Sitte established in the 1890s is capable of current interpretation. Decoration and ornament when used at the scale of a city is by its nature costly. There must, therefore, be a rationale for the use of decoration in some locations and not in others. Following Sitte's principle it is possible to envisage a hierarchy of locations for, in particular, publicly funded city ornament. Each city, quarter or district has its centre, the most important node in the area, where decoration would be concentrated and where its use would be encouraged. Other less important spaces in the hierarchy would not be so well endowed with funding for public art.

Location of decoration on façades in squares follows many of the principles so far outlined but the concentration of such ornament to particular positions in the square depends upon the physical properties of the space. A useful guide to those properties and, therefore, a useful tool in deciding the appropriate scheme of decoration for the square, is outlined in the typology of urban space developed by Zucker (1959). Zucker was able to distinguish five main types of city square: the closed square; the dominated square; grouped squares; the nuclear square and the amorphous square.

Before discussing the principles governing the decorative treatment for each of Zucker's type of square it is important to note the location where decoration should be avoided. Sculpture, fountains

2.26

2.27

Figure 2.26 Piazza SS Annunziata, Florence
Figure 2.27 Place Royale, Paris

and other city ornaments should not be placed against highly decorative façades. Such city ornaments are best seen against a neutral or plain ground. The corollary is true. A decorative or highly sculptural façade should not be placed behind existing ornate public monuments. This is the place for restraint in decoration, a point which is true of all types of square distinguished by Zucker.

Three good examples of the enclosed square as defined by Zucker are the main square in Salamanca; the Piazza Annunziata in Florence, and the Place Royale in Paris. The properties of this spatial type have been discussed elsewhere (Moughtin, 1992), but for the discussion of the decorative treatment of its façades the following properties seem particularly important. The space is static and normally of simple geometric plan shape. To emphasize, support and complete this static sense of repose the eaves line should be a constant or near constant height. This is not the place for exaggerated silhouette, asymmetrical towers or playful bays. In the main square in Salamanca a slight emphasis of roof line in the centre of the façade pinpoints an important function and the exit from the square. For the rest of the square the roof zone is terminated by a bold cornice. In this spatial type the treatment of the ground zone is particularly important. In each of the examples used here the ground floor is a simple arcade: on three sides in Florence and four in Salamanca and Paris. The repetitive rhythm and the deep shading behind the arcade completes the sense of repose (Figures 2.26 and 2.27).

The dominated square is one which has a directional emphasis, usually towards a building but sometimes towards a space, as, for example, in the Campidoglio, Rome. Sitte, like Zucker, also analysed the dominated square, he distinguished two types of dominated square. The first type fronts a tall building such as a church. The shape of the square is deep to reflect the proportions of the dominant building. The second type Sitte described as wide (Figure 2.28). It is placed in front of a relatively long and low building such as a Palace. The plan shape of the square or piazza reflects the proportions of the dominant building. In both cases it is the dominant building which should receive the most attention in terms of decorative treatment. The medieval cathedral is a good model for a dominant building in a square. The great west front of the cathedral towers before the observer with rows of statues in tiers of arcading, resting on the three main portals of receding recessed arches. It is in complete contrast to the pleasant small scale architecture with few decorative elements that encloses the other sides of the space. There is no doubt which is the important façade. The shape and directional quality of the space and the decorative treatment of the façade proclaim the dominant order of the space and also the society that built the city.

Linked squares, as described by Zucker, are often arranged around a particular building or those spaces in close proximity and linked by passages and arcades. St Mark's in Venice is a particularly fine example of a building surrounded by linked squares. In a case such as this it is the linking feature, St Mark's Basilica which is the element which is highly decorative. St Mark's is common to both the piazza and piazzetta and as such dominates the composition by its form and the wealth of architectural decoration. The roofline of St Mark's with its domes and pinnacles distinguishes it from, and contrasts it with the horizontal treatment of the Doges Palace and the buildings surrounding the Piazza including the library by Sansovino (Figures 2.29 and 3.12).

The nuclear or centralized square is one, according to Zucker, where a central feature is large and dominating enough to hold a space together around it by centrifugal force alone. A good example is Piazza di SS Giovanni e Paulo, in Venice. It is an ill-defined space very loosely enclosed by irregular buildings. The space, however, is held together by the central feature of Verrocchio's equestrian statue. In this and similar cases the success of the square depends not only upon the bulk of the central

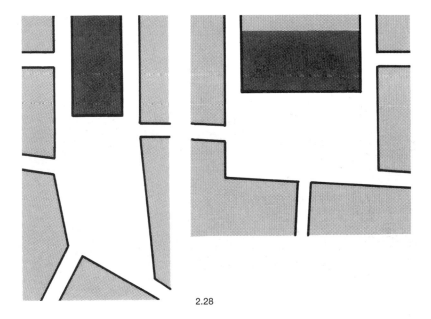

2.28

2.29

Figure 2.28 Examples of Sitte's archetype 'deep' and 'wide' squares

Figure 2.29 Doges Palace, Venice

2.30

2.31

Figure 2.30 Piazza di SS Giovanni e Paulo, Venice
Figure 2.31 Trafalgar Square, London

feature but also upon the power of its modelling or the symbolism of its shape. The walls of the space in contrast take on a secondary role where decoration is subdued. The wall of the hospital emphasizes this almost negative role using *trompe l'œil* to destroy the apparent physical boundary of the square, extending it by the subtle use of false perspective (Figure 2.30).

The amorphous square as the name implies has little or no shape. It may, in fact, be a square in its earliest development, or the buildings that surround a traffic roundabout. In the latter case decoration of any sort is wasted in a position where it will not be seen and in the former only time will tell where if at all, decoration should be used. Zucker cites Trafalgar Square as an amorphous space. He believes that Nelson's Column is not massive enough to hold this great place together (Figure 2.31). To a large extent it is merely a traffic gyratory system. There are, however, small places in the square itself and on its periphery where pedestrians can stop and admire decoration. The area in front of the extension to the National Gallery is such a place and, therefore, the location for a decorative façade. Some would criticize the recent extension of the Gallery as bland and not decorative enough.

The square, like the street, can also be studied in terms of its main function. Cities usually have civic squares, commercial squares and residential squares, each of which exhibit different approaches to decoration. The civic square is where we find the tragic scene as defined by Vitrivius. In the civic square façades are usually restrained and classical, designed to impress. The most important concern in decorating is achieving unity and rhythm. Campidoglio and St Peter's Square are two excellent examples in Rome. Commercial squares, on the other hand, are often examples of the comic scene, displaying exuberance through a variety of decorated façades. Even the most restrained commercial squares display a variety of types and styles of ornament and decoration. Commercial squares are also the squares where decoration is

2.32

2.33

more likely to change over time, expressing the fashions of different periods. Market Square in Nottingham is a good example of a commercial square where different approaches to façade decoration and articulation can be seen - classical, whimsical Victorian and unadorned post-war Modern (Figures 2.32 and 2.33). On the other hand, very often, the residential squares, unlike residential streets, tend to display tragic scenes - restrained façades decorated by unity and rhythm of small cues.

Residential squares in London, Bath, Edinburgh and Dublin provide good examples of squares defined by façades that are highly restrained and controlled. Arguably, the bourgeoisie inhabiting these squares preferred classical façades as they would give their homes added status by emulating the residences of the aristocracy and civic buildings. In the four cities listed above façades defining the residential squares again use unity and rhythm as the main control for decoration. Classical façades often use large elements and Georgian façades use small elements but the resulting unity is similar. In squares surrounded by classical façades the juxtaposition of trees and buildings often gives the impression of a more human scale, whereas Georgian façades do not require trees to create human scale (Figure 2.34).

CONCLUSION

The building façade is the feature of the urban realm where the appropriate use of ornament and

Figure 2.34 Bedford
Square, London

2.34

decoration is vital to the creation of a rich and interesting environment. Bland building frontages

without interest can be relieved by good floorscaping, the placing of fine street ornaments and by landscaping but these features can never be a complete compensation. The richness of the medieval and early Renaissance city in Italy is dependent as much on a highly decorative architecture as it is upon the wonderful urban spaces to be found in those cities. There must, however, be a rationale for the decorative design of urban façades. This rationale, it is argued here, is developed from an understanding of the way in which we look at buildings and from the best traditions of urban decoration. That is, from periods in the past when designers interpreted instinctively the principles of perception and produced great cities such as Venice and Florence. The two main components of the city where façade treatment is particularly important are the street and the square. While these two elements share many of the principles that determine the appropriate location of ornament there are important differences which derive from their different roles as path and node.

THE CORNER

INTRODUCTION

The design of the corner where two planes meet is a visual problem giving scope for expression in the design of almost any artefact, the design of the urban scene is no exception to this rule. Indeed, the handling of the corner is often an indication of the quality and mastery of the designer. To recognize the importance of a corner site and give it significance is to enrich the visual environment and the urban townscape. The corner, because of its significance, has often been an important element on which to bestow formal ornament or more personalized decoration: this, however, has not always been so. During the early period of modern architecture corner treatment was stark and unadorned. There have, however, been other times when the corner was not celebrated: many fine Georgian buildings in Britain, for example, presented the transition of planes at the corners of buildings simply with quoin details in materials which differed from those of the general façade (Figure 3.1).

While the question of embellishment of corner details is a matter of style, it is nevertheless possible to distinguish two generic types of corner: the 'internal corner' where two planes meet and tend to

Figure 3.1 Quoined corner, Regent Street, Nottingham

3.2

Figure 3.2 Parthenon, Athens
Figure 3.3 Internal corner of the Palazzo Medici – Riccardi, Florence

3.3

enclose space and the 'external corner' where two planes meet and present a three dimensional view of the building. The first type is most commonly found in the public place or piazza and the second will mark the junction of streets.

The importance of the corner as a node of pedestrian activity is often reflected in residential areas by the location there of corner shops and public houses. Until after the Second World War, the angled plot at street corners was considered choice terrain much sought after for private mansions, large luxury stores, panoramic apartment blocks, and prestige banks. These corner activities and the buildings which enclose them are often a counterpoint to less prestigious neighbouring buildings. This was frequently reflected in more elaborate ornamental work to mark the corner.

The art of turning the corner is an aspect of town design which frequently exercised the minds of builders in the generations prior to the so called 'Heroic Age' of the Modernists. This problem of turning the corner, in its most fundamental form, is expressed in the method used to resolve the junctions between gable and flanking walls of the megaron type structure common in countries with a northern European climate. The solution to many problems of building design often have their origin in the Hellenic period. The Greeks of classical times resolved this particular problem by taking the entablature round all façades of the building and by returning, at an angle, part of the flanking cornice to enclose and edge the tympanum of the gable. The columns supporting the gable were returned round the flanking walls enclosing an external ambulatory or covered colonnaded walkway, the peristyle. All four walls of the typical temple were unified by the repetition of the column theme supporting a common entablature and supported on three steps. The corner of the building is formed by a typical column with symmetrical base, shaft and capital (Figure 3.2). The early Renaissance architects also favoured a simple formula for turning the external corner relying upon a flat pilaster or rustically expressed quoin stones. More exuberant expressions of the corner are exhibited in baroque buildings where transition from plane to plane is prefigured in a ripple of pilaster upon pilaster. In Victorian and Edwardian Britain those architects taking their cue from medieval form gave expression to the corner using the tower or cluster of towers. The internal angle, while not possessing the same scope for expressive design, also presents design problems for the creative artist. The arcaded courtyard where arches meet at an internal corner can appear structurally or visually weak, or clumsy in the extreme (Figure 3.3).

So far corner design has been discussed at the scale of the single building. While for those practising urban design architectural analogy is important, nevertheless, for the purposes of this discussion, the building in its townscape setting is of greater relevance. In addition the townscape setting gives the corner an added dimension and scope for imaginative treatment. The street corner when given emphasis with decorative treatment becomes memorable in the mind of the viewer. It thus takes on added significance, performing the role of landmark. As such it is significant in strengthening the imageability of the city. A further function of the corner is its role in unifying two adjacent façades often acting as a vertical foil or contrasting element to the horizontality of the street scene.

THE CORNER TYPOLOGIES

Post-modern theoretical developments in architecture and urban design have frequently sought inspiration from historical precedent. Often these lines of enquiry have led to the construction of typologies (Krier, 1979; Rossi, 1982). A type can be defined as a characteristic specimen or illustration of a class or group of objects. The following typology of urban corners is one of physical types, a classification based on physical form rather than usage or function. This interest in the identification of spatial types and the construction of typologies has stemmed from the study of traditional urban forms as a reaction to Modernist approaches to urban form and design. The interest in typologies, however, is not a new concern. Zucker, for example, in his book *Town and Square* (1959) defines spatial archetypes for the analysis of urban squares. Zucker's typology is based on the subjective impression of spatial quality and is entirely independent of the specific function of that space.

The construction of a typology involves identifying common characteristics among the set of objects studied. In other words, for the purpose of this study, corners as they are used and appear in the townscape must be capable of arrangement in subgroups. For the typology to be of use it should have the capacity both to analyse existing situations and to act as a design tool. The purpose of the present typology is to assist the urban designer with the task of decorating the city. For this purpose the individual categories identified are relatively distinctive and discrete while, it is hoped, they are not so general as to be meaningless. The aim of this typology is to be both comprehensive and complete without the use of a 'catch-all' category into which all odd or maverick corners defying definition are neatly swept. As with any typology it is difficult, if not impossible, to draw precise boundaries between archetypes, and since this study is based largely upon historical precedent, new and evolving forms of corner may not fit within its parameters.

There are two typologies of corners: one for street or 'external corners', the other for piazza or 'internal corners'. Figures 3.4 and 3.5 illustrate each typology in diagrammatic form. The street corner can be categorized as: the negative corner; the angular corner; the curved corner and the towered corner. The last three categories can be further sub-divided. The angular corner can take the form of

Figure 3.4 Street corner
typology
Figure 3.5 Piazza corner
typology

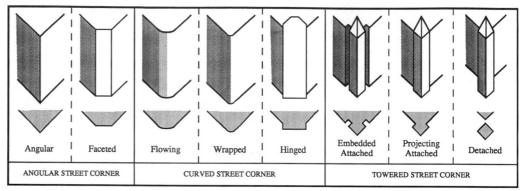

3.4

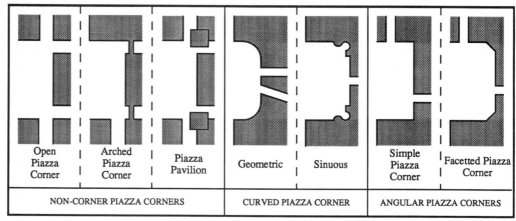

3.5

a simple angle corner, or be a faceted corner. Within the curved corner type it is possible to distinguish three sub-types: 'flowing', 'wrapped' and 'hinged' corners, while the towered type can be 'attached' or 'detached'. The piazza, that is, the space-enclosing corner, can be categorized as: the non-corner, the curved corner and the angular corner. Each of these categories can be subdivided into further recognizable types. The non-corner occurs where the flanking buildings do not in fact meet to form a junction: such corners can take three main forms: 'open', 'arched', or 'pavilion'. The

curved piazza corner can be either 'geometric' or 'sinuous' while the angular piazza corner, probably the most common corner for a public square, may be a simple internal corner or a more complicated faceted corner.

THE STREET CORNER TYPOLOGY

THE NEGATIVE STREET CORNER
Post-Second World War designers, have tended to ignore the problem of the street corner. A survey in

Brussels found that 'architects and public powers neglected the treatment of corners which are now systematically denied or destroyed' (Murdock, 1984). The authors of this survey suggest that the neglect of the corner imperils the traditional urban structure and is one reason for the city centre having the appearance of a slum. These strong views about Brussels hold true for many cities throughout Europe. One reason for the dismissive treatment of corners may have arisen from the imposition of engineering sight lines but this requirement was also supported by the urban philosophy of the day with its lack of respect for traditional urban spatial arrangements, streets, squares and the urban block.

As Le Corbusier, (1967) wrote: 'Our streets no longer work. Streets are an obsolete notion. There ought to be no such thing as streets; we have to create something that will replace them.' The negative corner takes the form of two buildings with gables exposed exhibiting the three dimensional form of both abutting buildings. The re-entrant corner is often a wasteland or it may be decorated with planting or murals painted on the gables. Often it becomes an ideal location for large advertisement hoardings. There is a need for strongly defined corners to establish the form of the urban street block, therefore, the negative corner is not recommended here as being suitable treatment for the meeting point of streets. It is included to establish a complete coverage for the typology.

THE ANGULAR STREET CORNER

The types of corner subsumed under this general heading are usually associated with buildings of the Modern Movement. The junction of walls, while giving emphasis to the expressive possibilities of the corner, nevertheless have been consciously designed: they are not, like the negative corner, the result of neglect. They are a response to the belief that the unadorned meeting of planes on a vertical line results in the most pleasing appearance for such a junction. Such corner types are not usually associated with ornament or decoration.

Figure 3.6 The faceted corner: Glasshouse Street, London

(i) The Simple Angular Corner

This sub-type arises when two street façades meeting at a corner join to form an unadorned sharply defined line. The façades may or may not join at ninety degrees. In this case the corner is often of less importance than the two façades, and in many instances is given no additional recognition or special decorative treatment. The different or similar design of the two façades may indicate or reflect the two streets coming together being of different or equal importance. This corner type is less than ideal where shop fronts are required on the corner of both façades.

(ii) The Faceted Corner

This design type is a primitive attempt to come to terms with the functional and expressive requirements of the corner while retaining 'modern lines' and a machine finish. The angle of the corner in this sub-type is simply chamfered, which improves the sight lines for the traffic engineer and resolves the difficulty of arranging shop window and/or entrance on the corner (Figure 3.6).

3.7

3.8

Figure 3.7 The flowing corner: Market Street/ Upper Parliament Street, Nottingham
Figure 3.8 The wrapped corner: Long Row, Nottingham

THE CURVED STREET CORNER

The corner types within this broad category arise where the two street-facing façades meeting at the corner do not meet at an angle, but instead the change of direction is negotiated through a curve. There may be strong horizontal elements which suggest that the building flows around the corner, or strong vertical elements which emphasize the corner as a distinct design element in the street frontage.

(i) The Flowing Corner

A flowing corner is one where the whole building frontage forms the corner. The curve is gentle, the corner is almost imperceptible, and can be emphasized using simple decorative features such as projecting eaves, string course or curving shop fascia. Cutaway ground floors within curving corners, unless carefully detailed and integrated with arcading or colonnade, can destroy the sweeping lines of this particular townscape feature (Figure 3.7).

(ii) The Wrapped Corner

The wrapped corner is also a continuous curve but the degree of curvature is much tighter than the last example. Strong fenestration detailing can be repeated from street façade to street façade encompassing the curve without change of rhythm. As a corner type it is most useful with deeply incised arcuated window forms where highly decorative and boldly modelled cornices and string courses subdivide the wall plane into flowing horizontal bands (Figure 3.8).

(iii) The Hinged Corner

The hinge can be a neutral method of linking the two street frontages or it can present an opportunity for embellishment which explicitly

3.9

3.10

Figure 3.9 The hinged corner: Shakespeare Street, Nottingham
Figure 3.10 The attached tower corner: King Street/Queen Street, Nottingham

acknowledges the additional significance of the corner. The hinged corner is similar to the faceted type except that in this instance the corner is negotiated by the insertion of a curved or faceted building element that is quite distinct from the street frontages forming the corner. Ideally the element forming the hinge should start at ground level and continue to the eaves: it is also explicitly differentiated from the neighbouring street elements by vertical setbacks in the wall. Linkage between neighbouring façades may be achieved by carrying cornices and string courses around the corner. The unified effect produced by these linking features however will be undermined if they become so prominent that they conflict with the general verticality of the hinge (Figure 3.9).

THE TOWERED STREET CORNER

The most powerful expression of the corner is the tower. Giving emphasis to the roof line or silhouette of corner buildings is one of the most successful and dramatic ways of turning a corner. Vertical impact at this important point in the urban scene can be achieved by extending the building façade beyond the eaves or parapet to make a strong elevated feature; the round or octagonal turret was a popular feature for this building element during the nineteenth and early twentieth centuries. This corner type is a useful focal point for a district or neighbourhood and is ideal as a city landmark.

(i) The Attached Tower

The attached tower may take two forms. In the first case it is embedded within the building fabric and does not project beyond the building lines of the

Figure 3.11 The detached
tower: Piazza San Marco,
Venice
Figure 3.12 Queens
Chambers, Long Row,
Nottingham

3.11

3.12

adjacent street façades. In this instance the effect of
the tower is achieved mainly by the projecting
turret, a splendid opportunity for lavish decoration
and dramatic silhouette. The second type projects in
plan and elevation from the building mass of the
street block. In this form the tower is more demon-
strative and assertive of its context and should be
reserved for those important landmarks that denote
the nodes which structure the city. The decorative
treatment of the projecting turret should be clearly
vertical with appropriate towered finish above roof
line (Figure 3.10).

(ii) The Detached Tower

This is probably the most unusual type of corner
treatment. In this case the tower stands in complete

isolation from the corner. It follows the model of
the tower in St Mark's, Venice, standing at the
corner of Sansovino's library and acting as the visual
fulcrum turning the corner between piazzetta and
piazza. As an urban feature where land is at a
premium the utility of a detached tower of this type
is strictly limited (Figure 3.11).

HYBRID STREET CORNER TYPES

Many of the basic corner types are capable, with
subtle changes of emphasis, of development into
hybrid types. The treatment of the roof line and of
the ground floor gives the greatest scope for invention and creation of the hybrid corner. In the case
of the street corner, in particular, they may be
layered and superimposed to create complex hybrid
types. For example, the building designed by
Watson Fothergill at the junction of Queen Street
and Long Row on the northern side of Nottingham's

Market Square is a simple angular corner type, where the roofscape expresses the relative importance of the two streets, but it also has the addition of a delightful stub projected tower element taking the form of a highly decorative oriel window (Figure 3.12). The treatment of the obtuse corner of the bus station in Tavira, Portugal deconstructs the corner element to such an extent that only a small proportion of the façades meet at roof level: the corner of the building being marked by a decorative column extending through two floors: both main floors are deeply incised. In many other ways the building is far from radical and complements the traditional waterfront of the town (Figure 3.13).

THE PIAZZA CORNER TYPOLOGY

The internal angle where two planes meet and tend to enclose space is most commonly found in the public square, place or piazza. According to Sitte (1901), the most important quality of the public place is its sense of enclosure. The public place or square is an outdoor room and together with the room it shares the quality of enclosure. The key to enclosure in the square is the treatment of its corners. Generally speaking the more open the corners of the square, the less the sense of enclosure, the more built up or complete they are, the greater the feeling of being enclosed. The internal corner of the public square is a townscape element which has not always been given great embellishment and, since its spatial qualities have been dealt with elsewhere (Moughtin, 1992), it will not be given great prominence in this text.

THE NON-CORNER
As the name implies the type of piazza corners grouped under this heading occur when the wall planes of the square do not actually meet: there is no actual physical corner. The sense of enclosure, the feeling of being within a place, is then determined and sustained, if at all, by some other method.

(i) The Open Piazza Corner
A prime example of this type of corner treatment is Michelangelo's development of the Capitol in Rome. One side of the piazza is a scenic platform presenting a panoramic view of Rome to the observer. The other two corners of the square, that is, between the Palazzo del Senator and the Palazzo dei Conservatori, and between the Palazzo del Senator and the Capitoline Museum are physically open but visually closed. The piazza holds together as an urban space because of the strength and unity of Michelangelo's powerful architecture and, secondly, because of the insistent decorative floor patterning which concentrates eye and mind upon the equestrian statue of Marcus Aurelius (Figure 3.14).

Camillo Sitte developed his own ideal piazza arrangement for a square with open corners. He suggested a plan form where the streets lead out of the corners of the square like the blades of a turbine, so that from any point in the square there is no more than one view out. He was basing his suggestion on medieval examples where he said 'in former days, if possible, only one street opened at

Figure 3.13 Bus Station, Tavira, Portugal

Figure 3.14 The open
piazza corner: Piazza
Campidoglio, Rome
Figure 3.15 Camillo Sitte's
'turbine' piazza plan

3.14

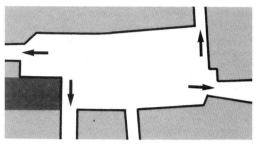

3.15

each point, while a second one would branch off
further back on this street and out of sight from the
plaza' (Collins and Collins, 1986) (Figure 3.15).

(ii) The Arched Piazza Corner

The use of an arch to connect the two adjacent
façades of a square is a highly decorative method of
closing an otherwise weak corner. The arch may be
placed within the wall of one of the square's
façades or, as in the Piazza Santissima Annunziata in
Florence, it may be placed a short distance along
the street and set back from the main space of the
square. Both methods of inserting the arch can be
equally successful. The arch itself is a highly decorative feature, an ornament of the city. Its potential
for framing a spectacular view adds a further dimension to the appreciation of the urban scene and
provides the urban designer with an element to
enrich the townscape (see Figure 2.31).

(iii) The Piazza Pavilion

Where two roads leave a square at the same corner
the gap in the public space can destroy the
enclosed quality of the square. It is the corner
condition most frowned upon by Camillo Sitte
(1901) and according to him, should be avoided if
possible. However, it is not always possible to
achieve ideal corner conditions for a public place.
Imperatives other than aesthetic conditions, such as
traffic considerations, may be of higher priority. In
Villa Real, Portugal, a small planned town of the late
nineteenth century, this particular corner condition
has not only been accepted in the main public
square but has been developed as an important
decorative feature of the square. At each corner of
the square four identical villas have been placed as
pavilions. Each villa has an external angle facing
onto the square which has been emphasized as the
main design feature of the villa and is the subject of
many decorative features. The four identical villas
complete the space in a most attractive manner
(Figure 3.16).

CURVED PIAZZA CORNERS

There are many notable examples where the
corners of a public place do not exist as such, the
place becomes a form of amphitheatre: indeed
there are several examples of urban spaces built on
the ruined foundations of theatres, amphitheatres
and gymnasia (Figure 3.17). The degree of

curvature for such spaces varies from the arc of the perfect circle to the gentler shape of the more complex curves. This type of corner, if it can be so termed has been used for the simultaneous design of several street corners in order to define an urban space. Whether it is the design of the corners which create the urban space is dependent on the size of the corners relative to the size of the space. In these instances the design of the space itself has often been more important than that of the surrounding buildings. For example, John Nash designed two circus spaces to define the crossings of Regent Street with Piccadilly and with Oxford Street. At the time both spaces were confusingly called Regent's Circus. They are now called Piccadilly Circus, where the circus is no longer evident, and Oxford Circus which was rebuilt between 1913 and 1928. In each case the circus was defined by four identical partially curved buildings on each of the four corners. Unfortunately the rebuilt Oxford Circus is weakly defined and its spatial qualities are now out of proportion with the scale of the streets forming the crossing (Figure 3.19).

(i) Geometric Curve

The paramount example of spatial enclosure taking a circular form is the Circus at Bath by John Wood the Elder (Figure 3.19). The Circus consists of three arcs of a circle: entry into the circus is at three points each on the centre line of an arc. The internal façades of the circus are decorated in three main bands or floors corresponding to three of the orders of architecture. The ground floor is decorated according to the Doric Order, the first according to the Ionic and the upper floor according to the Corinthian Order. The whole composition is finished with a band of solid balustrade which disguises the angle of the pitched roof. Other notable examples include the great colonnaded arms of the Piazza Obliqua, St Peter's, Rome; the Hemi Cycle at Nancy and the Exedras in Piazza del Popolo, Rome (Figures 3.20, 3.21 and 5.18).

3.16

3.17

Figure 3.16 The Pavilion piazza corner, Villa Real de Saint Antonio, Portugal

Figure 3.17 Curved piazza corners: Piazza Navona, Rome

Figure 3.18 Oxford Circus, London
Figure 3.19 The Circus, Bath

3.18

3.19

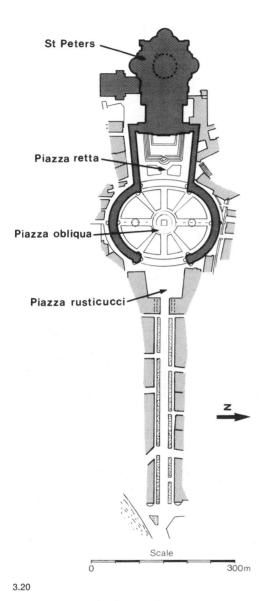

- St Peters
- Piazza retta
- Piazza obliqua
- Piazza rusticucci

z

Scale

0   300m

3.20

3.21

Figure 3.20 Plan of piazza
of St Peter's, Rome
Figure 3.21 The Hemi
Cycle, Nancy

(ii) Sinuous Curve

The Piazza of Sant' Ignazio in Rome by Filippo Raguzzini is the model for this particular method of turning a corner. In this small Roman Rococo urban space the earlier church and square are all part of the same unified spatial composition: in the development there is no clear cut corner, either within or without the church. Movement abounds, elements elide and overlap, façades of enclosing buildings assume sinuous shapes interrupted only for streets to mark the position of Borromini's church front. This is the ideal setting for urban decoration and for townscape to take on a playful theatrical role (Figure 3.22).

ANGULAR PIAZZA CORNERS

The angular corner of the square or piazza, like its counterpart the angular street corner, is not an element which is noted for its lavish decoration. Unlike the street corner where a great opportunity for lively ornamentation exists, a simple unadorned internal angle in a public square is apposite. The quiet and restrained corner permits the ornament and decoration on other more appropriate areas of the square to take precedence. The roofline at the corner of the square may be broken with sculpture or similar feature to recognize the change in

Figure 3.22 Plan of the Piazza Sant'Ignazio, Rome **Figure 3.23** Plan of the Amelienborg, Copenhagen **Figure 3.24** Street corner, Comyn Ching, Soho, London

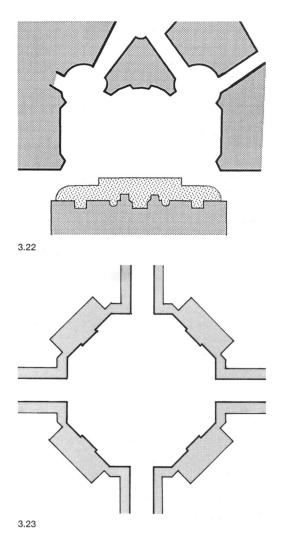

3.22

3.23

3.24

direction of the main wall planes, or a sculpture may be placed in a niche on the point of the corner. The corner is emphasized by the repetition of decorative features, such as arcading on adjacent elevations which dramatizes the visual function of the corner as pivot.

(i) The Simple Piazza Corner

This is probably the most common condition for the corner of a piazza meeting with the approval of Camillo Sitte as a positive space enclosing feature. Little need be added to the last paragraph except to note that the angle at which the adjacent sides of the space meet can be anything from an obtuse angle to 120° or more. At the large townscape scale the eye is not able to distinguish subtleties of angle and most resolve themselves in the mind to more or less a right angle.

(ii) The Faceted Piazza Corner

This type of corner can take the form of the multi angular Plaza Campo in Siena, where the lines of the building frontages follow approximately the older form of the Roman amphitheatre. Or it may take the more clearly faceted form of the north-west corner of the Piazza Navona which also followed the lines of an older Roman Stadium. The faceted corner can also take the geometric form of the Amelienborg in Copenhagen. The main square of the Amelienborg is the shape of an octagon with four identical palace buildings on four sides of the figure. Eight small pavilions attached to the main palace buildings frame roads entering the octagon on the remaining four sides of the piazza. In this latter form the shape of the piazza with its faceted angles is decorative in itself and promotes the possibility of further play with the corners to delight the eye and stimulate the mind (Figure 3.23).

CONCLUSION

The external and immediate urban context was not an issue of special significance for the Modern Movement designers. Thus the design of the corner as the junction of two defined elements of urban space was not considered as a prime design task or problem. However, with the questioning and rejection of the concerns of the Modern Movement, architects and urban designers are again looking at corners as important elements of continuity in the urban environment. Of the new generation of British designers, one of the most significant is Terry Farrell. He has responded positively to the corner as a design problem and his work such as Comyn Ching and Fenchurch Street, is comparable in exuberance to those of Victorian or Edwardian British cities. On the continent of Europe other well-known designers, particularly the New Rationalists, taking traditional city form as a source of reference, have explored the design problem of the corner. Examples include Aldo Rossi's design of the building at the corner of Wilhelmstrasse and Kochstrasse in Berlin's IBA and Mario Botta's office building in Lugano, Switzerland. (Figure 3.24).

The corner in town design, particularly the street corner gives great scope for the introduction of ornament and decoration into the townscape. While the embellishment of the public place or square is not so dependent upon the treatment of its corners, gaining its meaning and aesthetic quality from its shape, façades, floorscape and furnishings, the street scene is greatly enlivened by the treatment of its corner and junctions. The full expression and celebration of the meeting place of streets gives modulation, scale and rhythm to the appreciation of a city's urban fabric. If carefully handled, with due recognition given to important corners, the city's pathways and nodes will be enlivened with landmarks, so becoming more memorable for those living and working in them.

SKYLINE AND ROOFSCAPE

4

INTRODUCTION

The city skyline is a prime location for decoration. The skyline and its roofscape can be appreciated from many viewpoints. When viewed from afar the city appears in profile as a distant silhouette. The city profile is often most clearly seen from the arrival points, that is from the great city gateways or portals. Alternatively it may appear dramatically in view from highpoints in the surrounding landscape while from elevated positions within the city, panoramic views of roofscape are not unusual. From pavement level within the city, the skyline is appreciated in quite a different way. As the viewer moves about within the city, the roofline which encloses and encircles the streets and squares presents an ever-changing dark silhouette against the paler sky. Landmarks which may be remote from the viewer, the dome of a cathedral or the delicate spire of the local church, stand out from, and impose themselves on, the surrounding skyline. Such landmarks perform the main decorative role in the city skyline: they are the jewels in the crown, often emblematic of the city. Man's intervention between earth and sky is a powerful image of occupation, signifying a meaningful place in a particular locality

and having distinct form which makes manifest its *genius loci*. The decoration of the city, and in particular its skyline, can act as a collective symbol, something that represents the city and with which the citizens can identify 'it testifies that a group of people share a place and a time, as well as operate in close proximity with a good deal of interdependence' (Attoe, 1981).

DEFINITIONS

Skyline is a very recent term. Until the mid-nineteenth century the word skyline was a synonym for horizon, used in travel literature in reference to the meeting of sky and land (Attoe, 1981). Typical dictionary definitions are ' the line where earth and sky meet', 'the horizon' and 'the outline of a ... mountain range seen against the sky'. Use of the word 'skyline' in relation to buildings did not appear until the 1890s. Its new currency was directly related to a new building type, the skyscraper. Maitland's American Standard Dictionary of 1891 is the first known dictionary to include the word skyscraper: the meaning given is 'a very tall building such as now are being built in Chicago'

(Attoe, 1981). This intrusion of skyscrapers at the meeting of sky and land necessitated a broadening of the meaning of skyline. 'Horizon' being linear, horizontal and passive in form could not characterize the aggressive, vertical and thrusting form of man's latest additions to the landscape. Hence 'skyline' assumed this role and was redefined to include buildings seen against the sky. 'Roofline' for the purpose of this book refers to more local conditions: the outline of the roof or a group of roofs seen against the sky. 'Roofscape', a term which became popular in the 1950s and 1960s, denotes the landscape of the roofs seen from above in a panoramic view.

SKYLINE, ROOFSCAPE AND TOPOGRAPHY

For the purpose of skyline analysis two contrasting landscape conditions will be studied: the flat site and the hilly or undulating site. Clearly there are many sites which do not fall neatly into the extreme conditions. It is however these extreme conditions which will form the basis of the discussion to follow. There are also other landscape conditions, such as the extent of tree cover or the position, size, form and quality of waterways which are as important as topography for the consideration of city form and its decoration. While each unique and individual site will have its effect upon the skyline, the relationship of skyline and topography is nevertheless both direct and easily recognizable. The relationship of skyline and ground form is most easily established when studying the settlements built on flat or steeply sloping sites. Analysing these two contrasting conditions enables a discussion of skylines in settlements in areas of less well-defined landscape forms.

As a general rule formal or regular layouts are usually associated with a level site and informal or irregular layouts are a feature of a sloping site. The 'natural' way to group rectangular buildings is usually at right angles to each other unless there is

some overriding reason for doing otherwise. The result of this rational process is a regular layout on the level site. On a steeply sloping site groupings of buildings tend to become informal particularly if the contours are respected. In traditional hilltop settlements the effect of contours on built form is often very apparent: the roads and the accompanying building frontages curve following the contours assiduously, the whole town plan often spreading out with layers of development swelling outwards and downwards from the hilltop core like ripples on a pond. These general principles for normal or usual development on flat or sloping sites, however, require some qualification. Many towns or parts of towns that have developed on flat sites often exhibit irregularities in layout due to organic road design, ancient land ownership patterns and respect for existing features in the landscape. Conversely even in the most informal and irregular of hill top towns there often appears a regular structure underlying the patterns which have evolved. In the case of Priene, dating from the fourth century BC, a complete grid pattern has been implanted on the contours.

The most critical problem with sloping sites, particularly the isolated or visually independent hilltop, is the treatment of the summit and profile. A flat site, of itself, has no significance as a natural form, any visual interest depends upon the objects placed upon it. The hillside, in contrast, has a curved shape silhouetted against the sky: this curve of the hill, because of its form, is interesting. Contrast the pleasures of the drumlin country of County Down or the rolling landscape of the Derbyshire Dales with the uninterrupted boredom of some parts of Lincolnshire. An object placed on the ridge of the hill stands out in silhouette adjusting the natural profile of the landscape. Placing objects on the crown or ridge of the hill may turn an otherwise lovely shape into a jagged or serrated skyline.

There seem to be two main ways in which hillside development can be successfully treated. The development can be placed at the base of the hill or on its lower slopes. In this case the built form strengthens the base of the hill which rises above in an unbroken natural silhouette. When Maddocks, a nineteenth-century engineer and entrepreneur was siting a settlement on his reclaimed land at Traeth Mawr, north-west Wales, he placed Tremadoc, a small planned town, at the edge of the reclaimed land. It was in the shadow of the steep cliff-like edge to the flat reclaimed valley floor. In this case the hillside forms a magnificent unspoilt backcloth for the town nestling at its foot. The town's decorative skyline is the natural profile of the hillside while the outline of the buildings takes on the lesser significance of a roofline seen from vantage points within the town. More dramatic developments following this design principle are to be found at the great temples associated with the Pharaohs' tombs at Dier-el-Bahari in Egypt.

The second method of successfully dealing with a hilltop is to reinforce or strengthen the skyline by siting closely spaced buildings along the ridge following the original shape of the silhouette. The unusual relationship between built form rising sheer from vegetation below lends drama to the composition. The roofline in this case is a simple uninterrupted profile with few breaks; the roofline mirrors the landform from which it rises. When breaks do occur in this roofline they must be dramatic, such as a single spire or the grouped towers of San Gimignano (Figure 4.1).

When the hillside is covered without interruption by closely spaced buildings from base to summit then the original shape of the landscape is retained. If the whole composition is dominated by one great building, the landscape takes on a new dimension. Mont St Michel is a fine example of a landscape form developed to an extent where the original natural feature has been dwarfed and overpowered by the development. Such cases are examples of the 'grand gesture'. In the case of Mont St Michel, it is a gesture to the greater glory of God. The skyline with its ascending turrets and pinnacles is capped by a delicate spire, a formidable model for those

4.1

4.2

Figure 4.1 Towers of San Gimignano
Figure 4.2 Hillside town, southern France

Figure 4.3 Istanbul
Konstantinople

wishing to decorate the city with an ornamental roofline (Figure 4.2).

So far, the discussion has concentrated on the development of a single hill, the sort of development epitomized by the small Italian medieval hilltop city or the small housing cluster in the countryside. By contrast the modern city, and even some traditional cities extend over a wide terrain. Ancient Rome had its origins in the coalescing of seven hill-top settlements. Any of the approaches to built form so far discussed in this chapter are suitable for a city on undulating terrain. The hilltops in the city can stand out as green landscaped knolls above a general carpet of low rise development or the hill tops may be enhanced with high crowning developments associated with important city functions. To control, achieve, and maintain a skyline of concord and balance on undulating terrain has its difficulties, particularly where there is the means and desire to build higher than a uniform height of about four or five storeys. This has been possible in most cities since the last part of the nineteenth century. If the underlying topography is

not respected, then the city may as well have been built on a plain, thus denying the critical qualities of its location. In instances where cities have exploited the topography, the resulting skylines have given distinction to a unique setting. The quality of such skylines is not the result of the subtle placing of a single imposing building, but the result of a total built form in harmonious relationship with the terrain. Rome and Istanbul are two of the finest traditional cities where the topography and the city serve to combine to enhance the skyline. In Istanbul, for example, each of its seven hills is crowned with a cultural centre and a Royal Mosque. Each mosque has two to six slender minarets surrounding a semicircular dome. On the hill which dominates the entrance to the city from the sea is Santa Sophia and also the Blue Mosque. The grand scale of these monuments is in contrast to the human scale of the Topkapi Palace with its mini domes and scores of chimneys. In the low lying land beneath the seven hills stretches the rest of the city. This multi-layered composition defines a rich and imposing skyline (Figure 4.3).

The advantages of mirroring the topography with the roofline is illustrated in the *Urban Design Principles for San Francisco* published by the San Francisco Department of City Planning (Attoe, 1981). It is claimed that the 'near perfect' visual relationship of buildings and topography in San Francisco by the early 1960s was in part due to the 'hill-and-bowl' effect (Attoe, 1981). This pattern of building has two major advantages, first, from a distance the natural modulations of the terrain are accentuated, and second, views of the city and of San Francisco Bay from the hills are left unobstructed.

Some of the points made about hill-and-bowl development are illustrated in Figures 4.4 to 4.7 taken from Attoe (1981). Figure 4.4 shows that erecting low buildings on hill crests and tall ones in the valleys produces a uniform, horizontal skyline which obscures the topography of the site. Figure 4.5 shows that placing tall buildings in the valleys also reduces the visual impact of the hills. Figure 4.6 illustrates the preferred approach, the 'hill-and-bowl' effect, where tall buildings exaggerate the height of the hills and assure views for more people. In Figure 4.7 the point is made that if excessively bulky buildings are placed on hilltops, the hills are reduced to being just podiums for structures and no longer seem like hills. The only exception to the 'hill-and-bowl' pattern that city planners accepted in San Francisco was the cluster of tall buildings comprising the Financial District near the foot of Market Street. That concentration was considered, visually, an additional 'man-made hill'. However worthy these intentions, they were not able to control the development in San Francisco after the 1960s. As Attoe (1981) points out: 'Whatever had been distinctive about the light coloured city on undulating terrain was being overwhelmed by anonymous, highrise boxes built for profit and with no sensitivity to the San Francisco locale and its architectural traditions.'

The parameters structuring development on a flat site are quite different from those governing built form on a steeply sloping site. In some ways the

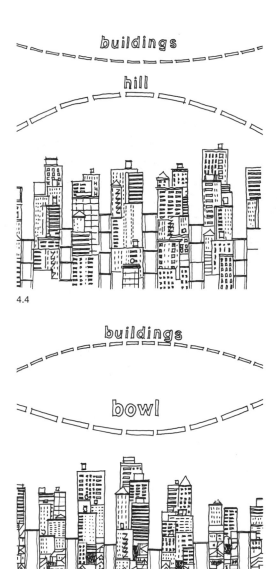

4.4

4.5

Figure 4.4 Hill-and-bowl development, San Francisco
Figure 4.5 Hill-and-bowl development, San Francisco

discipline is not so strict. The contours on the sloping site to a great extent determine the position of the long axis of buildings and also the location of

Figure 4.6 Hill-and-bowl
development, San Francisco
Figure 4.7 Hill-and-bowl
development, San Francisco

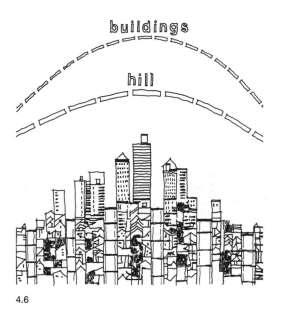

4.6

4.7

the main roads. On a flat site other criteria of a
practical nature, such as climatic conditions, building materials and construction technology, become
important for design. Unlike contours, however,
they do not have the same influence on the form of
the built environment. To some extent the designer
has to invent his or her own discipline for the

development of a flat site. The tool used for such
development is often the rectangular grid or linear
axial composition. The skyline form of the settlement follows and parallels the natural horizontal
horizon. In the traditional settlement on a flat site
the skyline may be broken by the contrasting vertical accent of a church spire. Generally, however,
the main decorative effect of the profile is experienced from within the settlement where highly
modelled rooflines and subtle changes in floor levels
break the monotony of the flat landscape. There are
few examples of pre-industrial settlements where
man has imposed his will upon the flat site with
expansive structures of extra-human or mega scale.
The 'cities of the dead' in Pharaonic Egypt are an
exception to this rule; the pyramid group at Gizeh
being the model for this type of development. The
massive pyramid tombs rising high above the
endless plain proclaims a new and gigantic man-
made landscape.

The older, central part of Paris was developed on
a relatively flat site along the banks of the Seine.
This part of the city skyline is dominated by the
Eiffel Tower. The Eiffel Tower is the prominent
mental image of the city; it is an image of Paris held
even by those who have never visited the city. The
Eiffel Tower stands for Paris. It is difficult to
imagine the skyline of Paris without its tower. The
knowledge that this great tower was originally
intended only as a temporary novelty landmark to
advertise the 1891 World Fair makes no difference
to this image of Paris. The city is overflowing with
great works of architecture, urban streets and boulevards that delight, but without the Eiffel Tower, this
wonder of the modern world, Paris as an entity,
would lack distinction. At a much more mundane
level, Blackpool without its tower and ballroom
would lose much of its significance for holiday
visitors. At great expense towers, such as that by
Eiffel and the much smaller replica in Blackpool, are
lovingly maintained and restored; their destruction
and removal is inconceivable. They are such powerful symbols of their respective cities, such important

decorative features of the skyline, that it is not difficult to imagine exact replacements being built, if by
some unfortunate mishap, their respective towers
were to fall.

In the USA there are several examples of grid
planned cities developed on flat sites. In
Philadelphia and Washington DC, where there have
been strict height controls, the skyline is much less
dramatic than New York or Chicago. The height
restrictions in Philadelphia were recently relaxed.
New York with a multitude of tall buildings has a
singularly dramatic skyline. The Chicago skyline,
which accentuates the 'loop' in contrast to the
lower development of the rest of the city, is rich
and dramatic with its cluster of skyscrapers (Figure
4.8).

The most dramatic view of the skyline is often
reserved for the main entrance to the city. This is
particularly true if the entrance is from the sea. The
contrast of a horizontal seascape reflecting the
colour of the sky with the waterfront buildings
rising from their mirror image makes this a special
scene in any coastal settlement. A notable example
of a city portal is the main gateway to Venice from
the Grand Canal. Entry to the city from the sea is at
right angles to the canal, between the Doges Palace
and the Library, through the Piazzetta San Marco
towards the Basilica with its highly ornate roofline.
From the sea approach the skyline is dominated by
the campanile. It is so important to the city and the
citizens' self-image of their community that it was
completely rebuilt earlier this century when it
collapsed. The medieval skyline of Venice is clearly
illustrated on the engraving shown in Figure 4.9.
The many church towers and spires reflect and
anticipate but never dominate the much greater and
more important Campanile of St Mark's. Liverpool is
another fine example of a coastal entrance. It is
dominated by a dramatic skyline. The three fine
buildings that form the immediate waterfront are
themselves dominated by the Liver Building with its
rugged profile and gigantic liver birds, the symbol of
Liverpool (Figure 4.10). Beyond, and proudly on the

4.8

4.9

Figure 4.8 Chicago skyline
Figure 4.9 Medieval skyline, Venice

Figure 4.10 Pierhead, Liverpool

ridge, sit the two cathedrals; both of which have highly distinctive silhouettes.

One of the most important decorative functions of the skyline is to facilitate orientation within a city. Tall structures of unique profile that stand out from the rest of the skyline function as landmarks. As Lynch (1960) defines them, landmarks need not be high-rise but those that do stand out on the skyline derive additional significance for the viewer. This form of city decoration can be regarded as simply utilitarian, an aid in orientation. As Attoe (1981) states, the skyline 'provides various kinds of information and in particular it provides information that aids in orientation . . . . This is the "landmark" meaning of a skyline, when it offers conspicuous objects that mark and identify localities within the city.' The Duomo and its campanile in Florence are an example of decorative skyline functioning as landmark: 'visible from near and far, by day or night; unmistakably dominant by size and contours; closely related to the city's traditions, coincident with the religious and transit centre; paired with its campanile in such a way that the direction of view

can be gauged from a distance' (Lynch, 1960). However, with the increase in the vertical scale of cities in the modern period, the legibility function of skyline decoration has become less straightforward. Thus there have been efforts to control the city skyline, to retain the historic skyline of cities by imposing a height limit on all but a few important buildings, or by protecting certain 'view corridors' from particular points within a city towards important buildings and skyline landmarks.

SOCIAL, ECONOMIC AND POLITICAL CONTEXT

The skyline is the crown of the city. The form and shape of that crown, its overall meaning and the symbolic power of its parts develops over the centuries. Urban form, and the skyline, can be considered the physical manifestation of man's culture. That is, the form of the city is a result of the way in which society, at any given moment, organizes itself in a particular location. Culture in the modern world, that is the social, economic and political structures of a community, the way it organizes and administers itself, the technology it employs and the values it holds, is not static. Urban form, together with its skyline, is forever adapting to these changes. Understanding the present decorative impact of the skyline, or more importantly, assessing the potential for its further development, are both dependent upon a knowledge of the history of cultural development. Historical insight and sensitivity towards the process of skyline development are important prerequisites for successful changes to city profile. Until recently in European cities religious buildings dominated the skyline. In the USA and increasingly in European cities, it is the commercial buildings which now dominate and define the skyline.

THE TRADITIONAL CITY
The skyscraper is the symbol of the new urban scale of the twentieth century. It was the result of

developments in the late nineteenth and early twentieth centuries. Prior to the nineteenth century, the size and scale of cities were constrained by the limitations imposed by both construction methods and available building materials. There were limits to the loads placed on traditional walls of stone and brick, limits to the spans of floors and roofs in timber. In addition the height and spread of development was limited by the restrictions of pedestrian and animal transportation.

Only in exceptional circumstances were buildings taller than the distance people would reasonably walk upstairs on a regular basis. Similarly the distance between workplace and home was only the distance that could be reasonably commuted on foot or on horseback. Tall buildings appeared in cities prior to the modern period, for example the Mesopotamian ziggurat was a great mound of development and the multiple towers of medieval Italian towns, such as San Gimignano, presage the romantic skyline of New York. There was also an increase in the vertical scale of urban development from medieval and early Renaissance cities to those of the Baroque. Morris (1972) notes that: 'In the old medieval scheme, the city grew horizontally; fortifications were vertical. In the Baroque order, the city confined by its fortifications, could only grow upward in tall tenements, after filling in its rear gardens.' Nevertheless, people did not commonly live or work at heights above four or five storeys. Tall buildings, apart from watchtowers, were used only for ceremonial and symbolic purposes. The result was a city skyline decorated with domes, spires, towers and minarets. To build high in the traditional city was a great undertaking, few buildings had patrons of sufficient social, political, religious or cultural status. Consequently, where such buildings occurred they represented and expressed the prevailing social and political order of that city. The skyline of the city is therefore the physical manifestation of how the city operated, which forces dominated there and what the residents valued.

The decoration of the skyline can be read as an index of cultural process and as the resolution, however temporary, of competing powers within society. Integrated to this dynamic balance are hierarchies of value expressed in the different modes of decoration and ornament. In Britain, in particular, city and state halls were domed to distinguish them from the rest of the city roofscape, while the many church spires indicated the special place of spiritual life in the community. Thus the traditional city celebrated institutional landmarks, buildings of communal importance having their *raison d'être* in religious and political power. As Kostof (1991) observes 'The source of wealth, of economic power, was itself sometimes institutionalised in representational buildings like cloth halls, with their stately towers proudly rising within the storied shape of the urban centre.' Siena displays a classic skyline confrontation between civic and religious powers. While the Cathedral with its command of fine decorative detailing assumes command of the dominant hill, the Palazzo Communale below attempts to overcome the disadvantage with its soaring tower. Despite the aggressive skyline competition of the traditional city, the boundaries of that competition were limited by construction techniques. The height of both ordinary and exceptional buildings was strictly limited. The manifestation of the competition in terms of the skyline was further restricted by the limited numbers of institutions able to enter that competition. The taller buildings, being relatively few in number, act as a vital counterpoint to the texture of the general urban fabric which was usually characterized by a greater degree of uniformity in the consistent use of similar materials and construction techniques. This is particularly true of the roofs which would in general terms be of the same roofing material, a similar pitch of roof with similar eaves, ridge and verge details.

MODERN CITIES

In the nineteenth century and more extensively in the twentieth century, the scale of urban development changed significantly. Prior to the nineteenth century, a building had been able to stand out or gain status simply by virtue of its relative scale and location. However, there was a growth and multiplication in the number of institutions competing for recognition and identity within the city. This competition was facilitated by developments in the building industry which increased the availability of imposing structures for those wishing to erect them. Towards the end of the nineteenth century and for all of this century the magnitude of urban development increased in both scale and presence. The consequent destruction of the spatial order in most traditional European cities is evident to even the most casual observer. Kostof (1991) sums up this development cogently: 'When the towered railway terminal and its hotel lifts up its silhouette in emulation of the cathedral, we know that the old values are reduced or overtopped. When the city centre ends up as an aggregate of tall buildings, we recognise that the city image has succumbed to the advertising urges of private enterprise.'

The most dramatic change came with the advent of the skyscraper. The technological inventions and innovations which permitted the development of such buildings were the safety elevator, invented in 1854 by Elisha Graves Otis, and in 1884 a method of steel-frame construction, worked out by the Chicago architect, William Le Baron Jenney, making very high buildings structurally possible and high buildings of all kinds much cheaper. The problem with high construction in brick or stone was that beyond a few storeys, loadbearing walls must be so thick at the base in order to carry their own weight and resist bending and overturning movements within the structure, as to make the extra floors so gained uneconomic. The advance of the steel frame was that it dispensed with this enormous mass of masonry construction.

The building of skyscrapers in the USA was an initiative confined largely to the private sector. Before the skyscraper boom, high buildings had been the privilege of the church or state, being confined to religious buildings and the palaces of those in power or holding public office. Over the last 150 years, height had become privatized and the property of those who could afford it. The users of the buildings extended to many in the community; people now lived and worked in skyscrapers and other tall buildings. The skyline, once the direct manifestation of religious or political power, now became the product of naked financial power – 'The skyscraper was a monument to the growing prominence of the modern American corporation. The corporate tower became the universal symbol of the city, and desirable for itself as proof of civic pride and prosperity' (Kostof, 1991). This translated into a civic desire to decorate the city with skyscrapers. While Henry James, returning to New York in 1904, lamented the overshadowing by office towers of Trinity Church – the tallest tower in the city until 1875 – the popularity of these buildings as civic decorations of a modern age was enjoyed by the city's population: as Kostof notes: 'In New York, people took the Staten Island Ferry to George Washington Bridge to see the city as the photographers saw it. Identifying the tall buildings became part of this ritual. Identifying the domes of Baroque Rome had been a tourist's ritual in an earlier era, and it was memorialized in the captioned Baedeker fold-out of the city's skyline as seen from S. Pietro in Montorio on the Janiculum, with St. Peter's at one end of the panorama and S. Paolo fuori le Mura at the other.' Despite the apparent glamour of the skyscraper and its appeal to architects, there was a resistance to building them in the older established cities of Europe. The resistance to the skyscraper is nowhere more in evidence than in the controversy surrounding the proposals for rebuilding the area around St Paul's in London.

CHANGING CITY SKYLINE:
THE CASE OF LONDON
Changing patterns of influence and their impact upon the skyline as a decorative element of the city

is clearly illustrated by the City of London. Until, perhaps, as late as the mid-nineteenth century, the skyline of the City of London was simple and dramatic: 'It was "cathedral on a hill", St Paul's Cathedral presiding over the town around it' (Attoe, 1981). The Cathedral, both in its original Gothic form, and later as the great Baroque masterpiece of Sir Christopher Wren, by sheer scale was able to dominate the merchants' premises and dwellings of the City of London. The later skyline was a combination of the juxtaposition of the rounded mass of the dome of St Paul's and the many delicate church steeples rising above the sea of tiled roofs and newly-fashionable chimney pots. As Attoe (1981) notes: 'Like cathedral cities elsewhere in Britain and Europe, the visual image of the City of London was that of a church-dominated community.'

This visual image of the City of London and its skyline remained intact for centuries, largely due to the limitations of available building materials and techniques, and by fire-conscious building regulations which restricted building heights. Post-Great Fire of London houses were generally of red brick and of a modest height of about three or four storeys. By the 1860s height limits had been raised in the City, and many of Wren's steeples began to be obscured by incremental development of office blocks. 'At the time of the London Building Act of 1888, building height was limited either to 80 feet or to the width of the street on which a building stood. The only exceptions to these regulations were church steeples and similar attachments. Even when new technologies - the steel structural frames, lifts (elevators) and fire-fighting methods - made highrise construction possible, height limitations were retained' (Attoe, 1981). The new urban scale was not universally welcomed. As Kostof (1991) notes, to make a point about the erosion of traditional values in the modern world, Pugin juxtaposed 'the new skyline of the industrial city, in England, a grim, stark silhouette of factories and tenements and warehouses, with the spire-pricked piety of the medieval cityscape'.

Figure 4.11 Office development, City of London

It was after the First World War, that the skyline of the City of London began to alter significantly due to the changing nature of business life in the city. An even more dramatic change occurred at the end of the Second World War. The intensive bombing of London had destroyed 27 million square feet of building, almost a third of the city's total floorspace. This wartime bombing was also responsible for eliminating some of the filigree of church steeples which, through contrast, emphasized the massive roundness of St Paul's dome (Attoe, 1981). Public sector comprehensive high-rise development, such as the Barbican, London Wall and Paternoster Square, was followed by a golden age for private developers as height restrictions were relaxed in the 1950s (Figure 4.11). More recently under the

Figure 4.12 Lloyds
Building, London, designed
by Richard Rogers

Paul's and though still evident, due to its unique shape, the Cathedral no longer dominates its setting as it once did. There is, however, a powerful conservationist lobby, orchestrated by HRH Prince Charles, which laments the passing of the original Wren townscape. Others believe such a viewpoint is idealist, even utopian. Change, those holding this view insist, is inexorable: 'For the Prince to presume he can go back to the seventeenth century city of spires dominating three to four-storey brick buildings is a regression in economic terms. We don't live in a Christian society dominated by the church, we live in a mercantile culture' (Jencks, 1990). If, however, the problems associated with finite resources, the effect of pollution on climate and world food shortages apply strict limits to growth then the search for more sustainable city forms will prove inescapable. In such circumstances urban forms similar to those advocated by HRH Prince Charles will not be utopian but necessary for the survival of city life (see Brundtland, 1987).

The changed skyline around St Paul's has been gradual and incremental. Although such developments have to be judged against the values, exigencies and imperatives of the period, they must also be judged against the universal principles of good design. The city of London is no longer a cathedral town. It is now an international commercial and financial centre. Should not, therefore, the skyline of the city reflect these important functions? Recognizing that urban areas are dynamic entities, not fixed once and for ever, does not invalidate the thesis presented here that each increment of development should be a positive attempt to decorate the city. Judged from this viewpoint, the development around St Paul's cannot be considered an elegant enhancement of the city skyline. The earlier decoration of the skyline was by shapes of an elegant form such as domes, needle thin minarets and finely tiered steeples. The modern skyline has been bludgeoned by dumb boxes and ungainly squat slab blocks. If the new office towers had been as distinctive and as distinguished as the older dome they

Thatcher and Major governments, a liberal *laissez-faire* philosophy has encouraged a more commercial approach where the height and bulk of buildings in a given location is determined to some extent by market forces.

The outcome of developmental pressures, particularly over the last 30 or 40 years, has been a reordering of skyline priorities. The hegemony of St Paul's has been successfully challenged. Post-war office structures have crowded the presence of St

Figure 4.13 St Paul's
Cathedral and the City of
London

may have been acceptable. The Lloyds Building designed by Richard Rogers illustrates what may have been. Unlike the Lloyds Building, the vast majority of new tall City buildings exhibit little concern for their role as ornaments on the City's skyline (Figures 4.12 and 4.13).

THE SKYLINE: COMPETITION OR CONTROL

A crucial question for urban design is the extent to which our city skylines should change as social, economic, technological and political factors change. The retention of a historic skyline by the conscious exercise of legislative and administrative control is common in European countries and also in Washington DC. Thus the decoration of the skyline is controlled by a public agency acting ostensibly in the public interest. Cities which have tried to control their skyline by use of an overall height restriction usually aim to maintain an established and historic hierarchy of building heights. The tide of change can be resisted by regulation,

planning and prohibition, but not always with success: 'St Paul's has not been lost, but its visual and symbolic impact have been contained and limited. The new role is very different from the old one. Its visual domination of its immediate environs is for the most part guaranteed through legislation and vigilance, and through recognition of its strategic role in London's tourism industry. But from greater distances - when it can be seen - it will be significant not for its massive presence, but for the contrast its shape makes with tower blocks nearby. St Paul's is no longer the symbol of the City, but the clue that this is London, and not someplace else' (Attoe, 1981). As in Paris, it is possible to maintain heights and densities by means of building and planning codes but given increasing development pressure such codes become increasingly difficult to enforce.

Explicit controls to retain the historic skyline of cities has been more a feature of European than of American cities. Washington DC is the one American exception: 'It is the nation's horizontal city, thanks to an unrepealed Act of 1910 which set

Figure 4.14 New York skyline

the maximum building height at 130 feet (39.6 m), similar to that of Boston and Chicago at the time. There is no mention in the Act of the skyline or the Capitol or any other monument . . . the Act has served the city well. Attempts by the real estate and building industry lobbies to revise the figure upwards have been effectively counterbalanced by the preservation movement, which fought to declare all of the L'Enfant plan off limits to highrise development and push beyond until the surrounding rim of hills' (Kostof, 1991).

The skyline of the contemporary city, particularly in Europe, is a negotiated symbol. The city silhouette is the official profile that is, in part, the result of a competitive struggle. Ultimately, it is licensed or condoned by state and city authority; it is a

political statement and as such its effect is simply the decoration that is possible in the circumstances. The skyline in the current political world is dynamic or chaotic depending upon one's viewpoint. It is continually changing, the result usually of the uncoordinated efforts of individual institutions striving to decorate and to put their own distinctive mark upon the skyline.

The harbinger of all modern high-rise cities is New York. Much of the dramatic effect of the New York skyline derives from the sheer concentration of tall buildings on a severely limited area of land constrained by the Hudson and East rivers. The skyscrapers of Lower Manhattan seen *en masse*, for example from the Brooklyn Bridge, present a dense array, seemingly squeezing all the space out between them like an early cubist painting. Despite the flat plain of Manhattan Island, the effect is that of a city on an undulating terrain, a series of man made hills, no doubt reflecting the underlying property values but analogous to shapes found in undisturbed nature. Unfortunately, the exceptional height of the twin towers of the World Trade Centre have introduced a new scale which dwarfs the rest of Lower Manhattan. Until they are matched by a number of other towers, the twin towers of the World Trade Centre will have introduced a dominance, one which the system of free competition they are intended to embody does not support. The hegemony the twin towers appear to suggest is at odds with the competitive vitality of the rest of Lower Manhattan (Figure 4.14). The effect of Lower Manhattan is repeated at Mid Manhattan. Here the Empire State Building, though the biggest building of the group, is better related to the heights of the surrounding buildings and does not suggest a dominant monopoly of space and power.

THE TALL BUILDING AS A DECORATIVE ELEMENT

In a traditional city skyline the uncontrolled, or uncontrollable, appearance of tall buildings, and in particular buildings of unusual shapes, detracts from the clarity of urban form and skyline by competing for attention with those buildings of ostensibly greater public significance. In the commercial city skyline, however, it could be argued that all means of distinction are legitimate. The Transamerica Pyramid in San Francisco, for example, is a building of unusual form (Figure 4.15). Originally a very controversial and unpopular building due to its distinctive and eye-catching form, it has since come to be appreciated by the citizens of San Francisco for its significance as a landmark. Attoe states that it is now used as a landmark for shipping in the San Francisco Bay area (Attoe, 1981). In emulation of Paris' Eiffel Tower, many cities have also attempted

Figure 4.15 Transamerica Pyramid, San Francisco

to build distinctive and unique 'status' towers - such as the Space Needle in Seattle or the Aerilon tower in Liverpool - that could fix a city's collective image. Not all of these have been effective. The skyline of Prague, for instance, is particularly disfigured by the 100 m high Zizkov television tower. Such buildings can be used individually to give distinction to the skyline, but their use *en masse* can trivialize. Arguably, however, what is more important than unusual shapes and forms, is the design of the attic and ground floor of tall buildings. It is these parts of tall buildings which are seen and experienced by people in the city. At its base the tower building forms part of the streetscape, immediately apparent to the passer-by. The top of the tower block is only seen from afar and, as the junction between the building and sky, it dominates the field of vision, from a distant perspective.

The decoration of the tall building or skyscraper can therefore be regarded as analogous to a classical column where both the base and the capitol have degrees of complexity, while the shaft is elegant and unadorned, its decorative quality relying solely on its graceful proportions. Among the architects who built the first American skyscrapers the man who really grasped the poetics of the steel frame was Louis Sullivan. It was his Guaranty Building in Buffalo, stating the lyric theme of soaring vertically, which became a feature of all later skyscrapers (Hughes, 1980). The top of tall buildings is a prime location for decoration. It becomes a means of bestowing distinction.

Of the two leading American cities of the twentieth century, Chicago and New York, it is New York which has always had the most individually decorative skyscrapers. As Girouard (1985) notes: 'It has become the convention to compare the stripped elegance of the Chicago skyscrapers with the columns, domes and spires of the New York ones, to the detriment of the latter. The difference in style in fact reflects the different situations in the two cities. New York was a head-office city and Chicago a branch-office one.' The New York and other East Coast investors who financed the Chicago skyscrapers wanted the maximum return on their investment, and thus required of their buildings a simple and 'stripped elegance'. However, when an impression was required the 'Chicago style' was rejected: 'All the early New York high buildings were designed to make a splash rather than to give the maximum commercial return. They were the headquarters of insurance companies, or newspapers, and of cable or telegraph companies which were often in competition with each other, and knew the value of height, splendour and a memorable silhouette in establishing their image or increasing their sales' (Girouard, 1985). Such buildings were in effect 70 storey billboards, a civic decoration but directed towards private rather than public ends.

The skyscraper as a dominant concept in city development may soon become history. If, as seems possible, this planet and its people seek a *rapprochement* with nature then sustainable development will become an overriding imperative for the city of the future. The aftermath of the Rio Conference and Agenda 21 has introduced a new realism into attitudes towards energy consumption, resource depletion, conservation, pollution and recycling. Certainly there will be no sudden revolution, no immediate cessation of the building of tall wasteful structures, and no overnight conversion to public transport. However, as finite resources near depletion, as the environmental costs of pollution and congestion are added to traditional development costs both excessively high buildings and low density urban sprawl will become less economic. The formulation of urban policies, under way in a number of European countries, that aim to reduce dependency on the car, encourage four storey high density mixed use development, organized in self-sufficient quarters, may have a profound effect upon the city skyline early in the next century. The model silhouette for such a sustainable or more sustainable city would have a form similar to the flat profile of the pre-industrial city; the high points of contrast being the preserved towers, domes and skyscrapers of former generations. Even in a more sustainable city, the skyscraper will probably remain as an anachronism of the past and perhaps as great a delight to the eye as Wren's spires and the minarets of Istanbul.

ROOFSCAPE

High buildings permit the city to be seen in quite different ways and from an altogether different perspective. Parisians were at first quite amazed by the view from the Eiffel Tower; that sense of joy and wonder is still experienced by visitors to the Tower. In a sense, each first time visitor to the upper stages of the Eiffel Tower experiences the city in a completely new and exciting way. The artist Robert Delaunay was so captivated with the view that he made a whole series of paintings of Paris exploiting this great vantage point (Hughes, 1980). The 'bird's eye' perspective or axonometric has become a common method of representing urban design proposals, but how many developments actually exploit the possibilities of roofscape decoration? Aronson's technique of the exploded aerial perspective with multi vanishing points is a most useful tool for recording and analysing public space (see Bacon, 1978) (Figure 4.16). Its emphasis on roofscape promotes the idea that this element of a city's public realm can be seen from high vantage points and therefore has great potential as a design feature. The delightful roofscapes of German medieval towns such as Rothenborg illustrate the obvious possibilities that roofs have as important decorative elements in the city scene. Nothing, however, is as depressing as the sight of serried ranks of flat grey roofs on a wet November morning. It should be remembered that the flat roof in the design philosophy of the architects of the Modern Movement was meant to be a delightful garden. The hanging roof garden may be an idea to which it is worth returning in an effort to green and decorate the city.

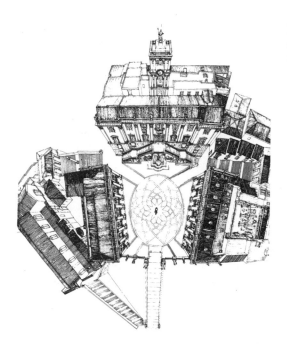

Figure 4.16 Aronson's aerial perspective of the Piazza Campidoglio, Rome

ROOFLINE

The roofline is that part of the skyline which is seen from the urban spaces within the city. Unlike the skyline which is a silhouette seen from a distance, the roofline, although also a silhouette, is seen from relatively short distances. The roofline is the profile or the topmost boundary of the wall of a street or public place; it is the meeting place of sky and building. As the edge of a main building element, it is a position where decoration has been traditionally placed. Since it is seen from close quarters, visual richness is important. This is far removed from the ideas of the Functionalist and Modernist schools of design; moral rectitude would impel the Modernist architect to finish the building façade in a crisp unadorned edge. A narrow plain coping stone covering a damp proof membrane would have been the sole recognition of this important design element. The unadorned curtain walled office block, unfinished at its edges, dating probably from the 1950s or 1960s, can be found adorning most city centres in Europe. Placing, on the roofline, ornamentation of sufficient interest and complexity, is one way of bringing interest to the modern city; it is a natural way to terminate a building and to celebrate the junction of sky and city.

Broadly speaking, there are four types of roofline. The first, which has already been discussed, is the plain crisp edge found in many modernist buildings. The second is the product of the natural growth of

4.17

4.18

Figure 4.17 Street scene, Rothenborg
Figure 4.18 Canal scene, Amsterdam

towns in the middle ages and is made up from a series of gables facing onto the street or square. The third is a product of the Renaissance, consisting of a horizontal ornamental edge to the building frontage. The fourth type is found in baroque building groups and advocated by the Beaux Arts movement. In this type, the roofline on both sides of the space steps up to the climax at the head of the plan.

Buildings in the medieval street had the long axes and ridge lines at right angles to the frontage. Storage was often in the roof space. It was serviced by a pulley beneath the ridge and above a shuttered door in the gable wall. Since plot sizes were relatively small, between five and eight metres, the gables fronting the street or square were sufficient to set up a rhythm and were close enough together to present a roofline of interest. Visual interest was strengthened because of the organic growth of the street, the variety of bay sizes and the different heights of buildings along the length of the street. Rothenborg is a delightful example of the medieval roofline, where a great variety of gable size is nevertheless part of a greater unity of style, colour and

material (Figure 4.17). The canal frontages of Amsterdam, with their variety of Dutch gabled properties, present this type of skyline over a large area of a bustling city centre (Figure 4.18). In the nineteenth century this medieval style roofline was adopted for larger scale office and warehouse blocks. It was sometimes used with a monotonous rigidity saved only by a wealth of detail. On occasions, however, the medieval roofline was used in the nineteenth century, with great sensitivity, by architects such as Watson Fothergill of Nottingham (Figure 4.19).

The Renaissance roofline returned to simplicity; its simplicity, however, was quite different from that adopted in this century by the Modernists. The models for the Renaissance roofline are to be found in the early Palace buildings in Florence. Buildings such as Palazzo Medici Riccardi and Palazzo Strozzi terminate with a great overhanging cornice supported on ornamental brackets projecting from a decorative frieze (Figure 4.20). The viewer is left in no doubt that the building ends in a profusion of decoration, including a deep shadow line, a deliberate exploitation of the Italian strong light. The insistent horizontal lines of the Uffizi buildings, terminating in deeply overhanging eaves, enclose the Piazza degli Uffizi in a manner typical of this roofline style (Figure 4.21). In later examples the cornice may be surmounted by a balustrade and further cornice, or ornamental attic wall. Distinctive shaped rooflines were reserved for the gabled front of the church or its domed crossing.

Baroque rooflines emphasize movement. The regular line of the roof is broken with towers and chimneys, and, in the case of Castle Howard, with

4.19

4.20

4.21

Figure 4.19 Castle Road, Nottingham
Figure 4.20 Palazzo Strozzi, Florence
Figure 4.21 Piazza degli Uffizi, Florence

Figure 4.22 Castle
Howard, Yorkshire
Figure 4.23 Queen's
House, Greenwich

4.22

statues and large ornate vases (Figure 4.22). The
scheme of ascending heights leading to the
dominant central feature on the main axis of the
composition lends itself to the celebration of power,
whether it is the power of the state individual or of
religion. Wren in his design for Greenwich was
defeated in his main purpose. The earlier placing of
the small scale Queen's House at the head of the
axis prevented Wren from placing there a structure
dominant enough to act as a climax to the roofline
of the hospital buildings with their twin domes
(Figure 4.23). As a celebration of power, the use of
this roofstyle by Lutyens in New Delhi was quite
apposite. Again the design was frustrated. The dome
of the Capitol at the head of the axis and the climax
of the composition sits uneasily in the background.
The foreground, on the ridge, is usurped by Baker's
twin domes over the less important secretariat.

4.23

CONCLUSION

The skyline, roofscape and roofline are prime locations for decoration. The skyline, which is appreciated from a distance, is dependent upon large scale buildings and towers dominating an otherwise generally lower and visually monolithic roofline. The main decorative effect of such buildings is the form of their profile. The buildings which thrust themselves through the general building mass should have interesting silhouettes. In the past, buildings with domes, minarets and towers have been the main decorative features of the traditional city skyline. Grouped towers in New York also have a romantic and attractive skyline reminiscent of the medieval town such as the multi-towered San Gimignano.

The roofscape is the sea of roofs that can be seen from high buildings or from other vantage points in the city. Such roofscapes present an opportunity for decorative treatment as landscape features in their own right. The detailed roofline is that outline of buildings seen from the pavements in the city. The roofline presents a changing profile of the city as the citizen moves around below. As such, they should be highly decorative and bring interest into the street scene. It is at this point between building and sky that ornament and decoration can be most effective.

THE CITY FLOOR

5

INTRODUCTION

The Campidoglio by Michelangelo has a magnificent patterned pavement of cut travertine in a setting of small basaltic blocks. An expanding pattern of stars emanates from the base of the equestrian statue of Marcus Aurelius. As the pattern flows outwards the star shapes interweave and ebb away like ripples on an oval pool finally dissipating on three raised steps which form the sunken depression within the trapezium formed by Michelangelo's three great façades (Figure 5.1). Walking the Campidoglio is a wonderful experience (Figure 5.2). The squares associated with St Mark's in Venice combine to form an equally stimulating visual treat for the pedestrian. Important to that visual and tactile experience is the intricate knot-like pattern of the pavement made from white travertine and black basalt (Figures 5.3 and 5.4). The pavements in the Campidoglio and at St Mark's, while quite different in form and pattern, have two qualities in common. Both patterns function as elements which unify space and give it scale. The pattern in the Piazza San Marco directs the eye towards the Basilica. The Basilica is further emphasized by the diverging lines of the square whose false perspective gives an added dominance

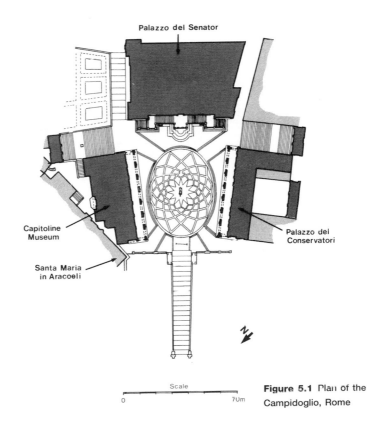

Figure 5.1 Plan of the Campidoglio, Rome

Palazzo del Senator

Capitoline Museum

Santa Maria in Aracoeli

Palazzo dei Conservatori

Scale

0   7Um

5.2

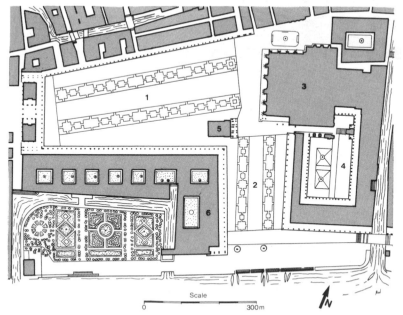

Scale

0   300m

1   Piazza San Marco
2   Piazzetta
3   St. Mark's
4   Doge's Palace
5   Bell Tower
6   Library

5.3

to this the main building of the composition. The lines of the floor pattern repeat the spatial theme and direct movement towards the Basilica. Michelangelo's pavement design for the Campidoglio links the centre of the space occupied by the equestrian statue of Marcus Aurelius to the enclosing walls. The sunken oval containing the pattern reinforces the centrality of the space while the expanding ripples of the central pattern emphasize movement to the edge and beyond to views of the city. Not all pavements in the city need to be as elaborate as St Mark's or the Campidoglio in Rome. Humbler surfaces like the quadrangles in Oxford and Cambridge have qualities which make walking attractive. This chapter explores some of the decorative qualities of the City's floor plane relating decorative quality to function.

The design and construction of traditional pavements has varied from place to place, very often being dependent upon the regional availability of materials. The decorative pattern of traditional pavements in city streets and squares is often richer than those of the recent past. Halprin (1962) describes traditional pavements as 'thrown like a rich rug underfoot'. Modern materials, however, can be richly textured and highly coloured. It is not the lack of material or financial constraints but the non-appreciation by designers of ornament and decoration when used on the pavement which results in modern pavements appearing dull and unattractive. Recent floorscaping projects in, for example, Nottingham have reintroduced pattern into pavements achieving an improvement in the appearance of the urban scene (Figure 5.5). Starting from an analysis of traditional city floorscape, this chapter aims to develop a rational set of principles as a guide to the use of patterning on pavements.

Figure 5.2 Campidoglio, Rome
Figure 5.3 Plan of the Piazza San Marco, Venice

5.4

5.5

Figure 5.4 Piazzetta, Piazza San Marco, Venice
Figure 5.5 Decorative pattern in floor paving, Nottingham

SCOPE OF STUDY

In the immediate post-Second World War period public open space was defined in terms of those areas used for sport, such as sports fields, or areas for more passive recreation such as the formal city parks. Outside the city, Country and National Parks completed the picture of open space for use by the general population. While not suggesting that open space of this nature is unimportant, nevertheless, such definition of public open space is a great oversimplification. The city's most extensive public open space is made up of its streets and public squares: this is where much, if not most, recreation occurs. When planning for the citizen's enjoyment of the city a holistic attitude is necessary: an attitude which defines city space from doorstep to regional park. Dealing with the planning and design of this extensive and complex spatial system requires of the designer, in the first instance, its organization into smaller units of study, bearing in mind, that it is the overall structure, organization and appearance which is of greatest significance.

The floor plane of public space and its patterning is the subject matter of this chapter. There are two main types of floor plane within the city: the hard pavement and the soft landscaped area. The soft landscaped spaces within the city and its region include areas of wild landscape, farm land,

Figure 5.6 Pavement, Pienza

ornamental pavements and traffic calmed areas of the city which are the subject matter of the following paragraphs.

THE FUNCTION OF THE GROUND PLANE

The main function of any paved area is to provide a hard surface. The function of a soft landscaped area is to introduce nature into the built environment. These functions of the two main methods of covering the urban ground plane are so obvious that the more subtle minor functions are sometimes dismissed as unimportant or are ignored completely. Beazly (1967), whose work is a standard text for the design of paved areas, states: 'It is a safe rule, though it must occasionally be broken, never to change the material without a practical reason. Today, the re-awakening of interest in paving materials has sometimes led to their use simply for the sake of textural pattern; the result can be very precious.' It is true that in many traditional examples of paving, the reason for change of material or for the pattern is the result of some very practical reason. The opportunities for a decorative floor plane resulting from such considerations naturally should be maximized. Beazly, however, was writing in the 1960s when the prevailing sentiment was for subdued ornament and an almost total reliance upon the functional creed as the justification and excuse for patterning. St Mark's Square, Venice and the Campidoglio in Rome exploit and celebrate patterning if not for its own sake then for purely aesthetic reasons. These examples are not isolated. Throughout Italy and the Iberian peninsula there are pavings of intricate beauty, truly the 'rich rug' beneath the feet (Figures 5.6 and 5.13).

THE PAVED SURFACE

landscaped parks, and ornamental areas of soft landscape set within otherwise hard pavements. It is this latter type of soft landscaped area which will be considered in this chapter. In terms of hard pavements, there are the heavily trafficked streets or roads and those that carry pedestrian traffic or a mix of pedestrian and light vehicular loads. It is the

The main function of a paved area is to provide a hard, dry, non-slippery surface which will carry the traffic load, both wheeled and pedestrian, without early disintegration. A change of traffic may therefore require a change of flooring material, and where this change occurs, careful use of materials offers an opportunity to create a decorative edge. The most common edge between vehicular and pedestrian traffic is the ubiquitous granite or concrete kerb with a drop in pavement level of ten to fifteen centimetres. If vehicular traffic is heavy then a double kerb may be an effective method of giving added pedestrian protection. Adding further parallel lines to the edge gives greater definition to the change of function and also added decorative effect. The kerbstone may be either upstanding or not, and a drainage channel can be added at the edge of the carriageway, in three bands of granite setts, for example. In addition, if space permits, a grass verge separating the pedestrian from the vehicular traffic (Figure 5.7).

Three practical functions of a pavement are to indicate ownership; to act as a hazard; or to give warning. Flooring material can be changed for any of these reasons. Patterning can be introduced when changing the flooring material and, if used consistently, a decorative rhythm is developed for the micro structure of the city. The floorscape has the potential to become a language which can be read, memorized and can impart meaning. The use of textured paving at road crossing points is essential to allow the blind and partially sighted to successfully negotiate dangerous points in the environment: in essence it is an extension of braille. As a concept it is just as useful for the fully sighted to negotiate the hazards of city life. Its use also adds a new aesthetic dimension to that experience. The use of setts in a flag stone pavement where a private road or drive crosses it to reach the street is a traditional and highly decorative way of indicating a hazard to the pedestrian. It immediately makes him or her aware that the pedestrian footpath ends (Figure 5.8). 'Ankle breaking' cobbles set in concrete is a modern technique to prevent pedestrians wandering onto a busy road (Figure 5.9). This use of cobbles,

5.7

5.8

Figure 5.7 Grass verge, New Earswick, York
Figure 5.8 Obstruction warning by textured paving

Figure 5.9 Hazard warning
by textured paving
Figure 5.10 Edging to
lawn

5.9

5.10

while having a similar function, compares unfavourably with the traditional and more subtle arrangement of two or three rows of cobbles between paved footpath and lawn (Figure 5.10). A change of paving material can be used to indicate a change of ownership letting the pedestrian know where the public realm ends and private property is being entered. This device is often used where a restaurant spills over, with its chairs and tables, onto a street or square. It is also used in front of hotels, banks and shops as a way of making the public realize that they are now on private property which is for the use of private clients. Devices for changing the floor pattern introduce a necessary element of decoration into the floor plane,

furthermore if that patterning attains a consistency over large areas of the city then it contributes effectively to its imageability.

Paving can be designed to provide a sense of direction or to give a feeling of repose. Both are aspects of the same function which is to guide and give meaning to the rhythm, pace and pattern of movement. At a very basic level paving can be designed to guide pedestrians or vehicles through an area where there may be few other indications of the route to be taken. There are many fine examples of stone slab footpaths set within a sea of cobbles: the stone slabs, for example, may indicate the route for visitors or strangers to traverse a semi-private courtyard (Figure 5.11). Paving slabs sunk

5.12

5.11

deep within a carpet of lawn play a similar directional role. A diagonal across a monolithic surface, particularly if the line of paving is edged and augmented with cobbles or setts laid parallel to it, introduces an essential element of decorative patterning, the fundamental basis of an environment with human scale. Directional paving may have a purely aesthetic function with no pretence at utility. It may simply be used within a street to reinforce the linear form of the space and so enhance the sense of movement.

The junction between the horizontal plane of the pavement and the vertical plane of the street façade is a line which in the past has been exploited for decoration. It is one of those important places in the built environment which can be celebrated by the repetition of parallel lines - the plinth, lines of parallel paving, the kerb and the street gutter. Parallel lines following the length of the street reinforce the insistent movement and carry the eye along the path to its termination. Unfortunately many recent pedestrianization schemes ignore this linear theme: the paving often running in an undifferentiated manner from one side of the street to the other without kerbstone or memory of sidewalk. Where patterning is used, as in the Broadway, Lace Market, Nottingham the result can look awkward and clumsy if the edging to the street paving follows a geometrical form other than the insistent line of the street frontage (Figure 5.12). Broadway is a sinuous street - the finest spatial experience in Nottingham. Unfortunately the recent insensitive paving has, both in design and execution, detracted from this space. The opportunity of repeating, in the paving pattern, the sinuous forms of the street plan has been missed, together with the opportunity of retaining the proportion and scale of the street by using raised pavements on both sides of the space.

Figure 5.11 Directional paving, Boston, Lincolnshire
Figure 5.12 Broadway, Lace Market, Nottingham

5.13

5.14

Figure 5.13 Public garden, Tavira, Portugal

Figure 5.14 Paving, Piazza del Campo, Siena

Paving designed to provide a sense of repose is usually associated with areas in the city where people stop and rest: it is the equivalent of pauses in music. It is used in places where people socialize, drink coffee, admire the view of a fountain, a sculpture or a distant prospect. The town square, or the nodes where people meet, are often treated as areas of neutral, non-directional paving. Such paving has the effect of halting people. Equally effective are patterned floors which can give a place a focus of interest. The centre of interest may be the pattern itself or some feature such as, for example, the bandstand in the public garden in Tavira in the Algarve, Portugal, to which the gaze of the onlooker is directed by the insistent pattern of the pavement (Figure 5.13). The interplay of floor patterns which alternate between movement and rest can be designed as the city's choreography, bringing qualities of rhythm, scale and harmony to the urban scene.

Some functions of the hard pavement in towns and cities are concerned with aesthetic requirements in contrast to those discussed previously which are either purely or partly practical in nature. These aesthetic functions include: enhancing the character of an area; retaining some connection with the past, that is, maintaining a memory trace; breaking the scale into more human and visually manageable proportions; signalling a change of design element or simply resorting to ornament and decoration almost for its own sake.

Successful paving reinforces the character of a place. It is part of the greater unity of buildings, soft landscape features, urban furniture, sculptural features, fountains and pools. The character of a paved area is determined partly by the materials used, be they brick, stone slabs, cobbles, concrete or macadam (Beazly, 1967). The edging detail is also important in determining the character of a paved landscape. The character can vary from the hedge-lined rural path to the highly formal macadam surface with precision-formed kerb. Materials, however, of themselves, have no singular unalterable character. This character of a landscape depends more upon the use of the materials, how they are arranged and how they interrelate with other materials and landscape features. A carefully designed floorscape can give to an area a unity which may otherwise be absent from a disparate group of buildings. The dish like pavement of the Piazza del Campo in Siena holds together the great volume of the square repeating and reinforcing the colour of the surrounding walls. The floor pattern is determined by the drainage channels which fan out from the Palazzo Communale towards the curving wall of the less imposing façades (Figure 5.14). Many traditional parts of other cities also have an overall unity of which the pavement is but part. For example, the brick pavements of Dutch streets echo the material of surrounding façades in one unified and highly decorative townscape (Figures 5.15).

In streets which are being pedestrianized the question is raised of the advisability of retaining pavements. The functionalist view would suggest that the removal of vehicular traffic from streets eliminates the need for a raised kerb and pavement as a vehicular and pedestrian separator. From a narrowly functionalist point of view, this argument is tenable. However, such a design strategy ignores the aesthetic requirement of enhancing the linear quality of the street which is an important consideration. More importantly, if this functionalist principle is followed, an opportunity to retain some link with the past is lost: the memory trace of past necessities is destroyed for ever. Towns and cities are full of such anachronistic and intriguing features which, some would suggest, lend enchantment and interest in an otherwise bland urban world.

Decorative patterning in pavements can perform the important aesthetic function of breaking down the size of large hard surfaces into more manageable

Figure 5.15 Paved square, Delft

human proportions. However, care must be taken when using patterning in pavements to manipulate scale. If not handled carefully, such types of patterning can look forced and artificial. The dished pavement of the Piazza Obliqua designed by Bernini as part of the setting for St Peter's, Rome, depends for its main effect, not on decorative paving, but on the dominance and grandeur of the colonnaded arms of the Piazza, the obelisk at its centre and two flanking fountains. The sweeping dish is emphasized only by eight radial spokes centred on the obelisk, otherwise the vast area has only the pattern of slabs to give it scale (Figure 5.16). In general, paving slabs of stone have a natural scale related to human dimensions. They therefore require no additional patterning for the purpose of determining scale. A pattern within a slabbed pavement may be necessary for other reasons but rarely for those of scale. Macadam or large *in situ* concrete surfaces, often need to be divided by some sort of patterning. Macadam car parks of great and faceless extent present a problem of scale. The division of large areas of car parking into small units based upon the

Figure 5.16 Piazza
Obliqua, St Peter's, Rome
Figure 5.17 Floor
patterning to edge feature,
Portugal
Figure 5.18 Figurative
paving, Portugal

5.16

5.18

5.17

module of the car space is essential if they are to be
humanized. Patterned paving accompanied by
judicious tree planting can turn a desolate 'wasteland' into a pleasant environment.

The floorscape can be enriched in a similar
fashion to the façade of a building by repeating and
echoing the shape of any element set into or onto
the floor plane, by emphasizing a change of material
and by dramatizing the edge of a paved area. In a
previous paragraph, the detailing of the junction
between façade and pavement was described. A
similar treatment is often given to the area immediately surrounding the plinth of a statue, the bowl of
a fountain, opening for tree or soft landscaped area.
Rows of cobbles, setts or coloured paving slabs run
parallel to the element, offering the feature to the
general mass of the floor plane (Figure 5.17).

By far the most difficult decorative effect to classify, analyse and suggest design principles for, is that type of patterning which appears to exist for its own, purely ornamental reasons: it is almost 'art for art's sake'. When there is some clearly symbolic reason for the motif employed, then interpretation is simplified. The theme of a cross on the pavement adjacent to the war memorial in Tavira or the depiction of sea creatures on the pavements of the fishing port of Villa Real de Saint Antonio, both in Portugal, are symbolic representations of this type (Figure 5.18). The decorative effects associated with towns in the Algarve are assisted by the nature of the flooring material – small black and white $5 \times 5 \times 5$ cm granite setts. The small tesserae of mosaic floors in the ancient cities of Crete, Greece and Rome lend themselves to an elaborate patterning and indeed demand such treatment by the artist. The floors of the Ancient World of the Mediterranean included both geometric and naturalistic styles of patterning. Exuberance in decorative floor patterning should not be dismissed too readily by those with a functionalist turn of mind, for whom ornament smacks of effete self-indulgence. The floor plane, long neglected by designers, or sometimes timidly exploited, is an unexplored subject awaiting the artist to express the highest values of twentieth-century urban life.

CHANGING LEVEL

The Spanish Steps in Rome is a dramatic design for a staircase, an elegant solution to a change of level, transforming a necessity into a pleasurable experience. Its articulated stepped form, with rhythmic variations broken by platforms where curving stairs meet like dancers of some stately minuet, presents, to Roman and visitor alike, a stage set of magnificent proportions. It is a place for children to play, the young to court and the elderly to sit and stare. These and other activities are the by-product of a design that delights in vertical movement enhanced

Figure 5.19 The Spanish Steps, Rome

by continuous flights and counter-flights of flowing curves: this is its primary function, but how beautifully has the Spanish Steps achieved several different objectives (Figure 5.19).

Steps, ramps, platforms and long sloping planes contrast with the horizontal plaza, the place for rest, conversation and meditation. By that contrast the sense of drama is enhanced. Emphasizing the variation in level, using ornamental staircase and ramp, adds to the quality and grandeur of the urban scene so that it does indeed take on the qualities of dance and theatre. Steps have, in the past, been used to dramatize events, to create places from which to address the crowds. Steps are places where tourists, beggars and street traders gather to pause for breath or ply their trade, or, as in the Campidoglio, a lofty height from which to view the city (Figure 5.20).

The primary function of the floor plane is to accommodate changes of level using means which are easy to traverse by both able-bodied people and also by those who are handicapped. The old, the frail and less able-bodied would find the Spanish Steps and the Capitoline Hill a daunting prospect.

5.20

Figure 5.20 The
Campidoglio, Rome
Figure 5.21 Plan of Piazza
del Popolo, Rome

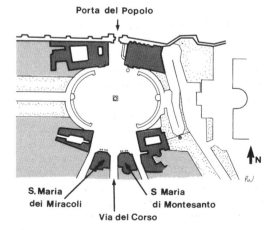

Porta del Popolo

S. Maria
dei Miracoli

S Maria
di Montesanto

Via del Corso

N

5.21

Special arrangements for negotiating changes in
level must be made for the handicapped.

Where steps are necessary for changing level,
they should be accompanied by a ramp for those in
wheelchairs or parents with buggies and prams.
Steps are not always the most convenient method of
accommodating a change in ground level. Ramps are
necessary not only for the handicapped and those
pushing prams but also for cyclists and where the
pavement is shared by pedestrian and wheeled
traffic. Where, however, the ramp is to be used by
pedestrians, it should approximate to a 1 m rise in
20 m: this is the most comfortable slope for walking
up and down (Halprin, 1972). The ramp, in addition
to its utility, has great potential as an ornamental
feature of the city. It establishes a quite different
aesthetic experience from the stair: it gives a more
insistent quality to continuous vertical movement.
Unlike a staircase, the ramp does not offer the same
opportunity to stand, rest and look about on
platforms between flights of steps. The fluidity of
the movement is beautifully expressed in the long
curving ramps of the exedra connecting the Pincio
gardens with the Piazza del Popolo, Rome (Figures
5.21 and 5.22).

SOFT LANDSCAPED AREAS

All paved surfaces have to be drained. Large surfaces
such as Piazza Campo in Siena and Piazza Obliqua,
St Peter's, Rome are dished, falling dramatically to
the rainwater outlet points. Even small surfaces have
their drainage channels and grids, which can be
highly decorative features of the urban environment.
However, dealing with the surface run-off of rainwater in a city is a major undertaking. It is also expensive, often involving engineering works. In addition,
the universal canalization or culverting of streams
and rivers represents a lost opportunity of living
with nature and ornamenting the city with decorative river walks. Natural areas have an important
role in the hydrological cycle of cities as well as

Figure 5.22 Piazza del Popolo, Rome

serving the needs of wildlife. Naturalistic open space, being permeable, slows the speed of rainwater run-off, so benefiting hydrology. Increasing the area of permeable land reduces the need to culvert water courses, a necessity only because of the large areas of impermeable city land and the consequent difficulty in controlling fluctuations in the water table (Elkin and McLaren, 1991). The use of load bearing but permeable materials for hard surfaces is useful in the attempt to modify run-off. Such materials are particularly recommended for car parks.

The present dominance of the hard impervious pavement in towns and cities is in part responsible for increased urban temperatures and lowered humidity. These micro-climatic changes in turn increase the demand for artificially controlled internal environments dependent on air conditioning. Landscape wedges linking periphery to city centre,

together with local green spaces in squares, on roofs and in private courtyards, can counter adverse local climatic conditions. The green lungs of the city trap particulates, increase humidity and limit the extremes of temperature to which buildings are exposed. Much of the landscaped open space in urban Britain is dominated by mown, chemically retarded grass, and a few scattered ageing trees. The degraded landscape is often the product of imposed financial constraints or popular dislike of unkempt, 'weedy' and natural environments. There is little money available for the maintenance and rehabilitation of many British parks - an important part of the country's heritage. The heritage of municipal parks was donated by city fathers of previous generations. It was a useful contribution to the ornamentation of towns and cities in this country. Sir Titus Salt, for example, when he built the small town of Saltaire, which at the time was completely

Figure 5.23 Lawn, Finsbury Circus, London

surrounded by rural landscape, still included a small municipal park as part of the development.

GRASS COVER

Conventional amenity landscaping - that is landscaping consisting largely of mown grass - is more expensive to maintain than other landscape types. Native landscape, established using largely self-sown native vegetation is by far the cheapest type of landscape both to establish and to maintain. Naturalistic landscaping is defined as creating new habitats to simulate native vegetation: it is the most expensive of the three landscapes to establish but is cheaper than the amenity landscape to maintain (Elkin and McLaren, 1992). Cost factors, particularly ongoing maintenance costs are not the only

justification for establishing native and naturalistic landscapes. They have their rightful place in the structure of a city's open space. Similarly conventional amenity landscaping should not be dismissed because of the relatively high maintenance costs. Lawns, colourful flower beds and neatly manicured bushes beloved by so many residents, are important city amenities and serve a most useful function in ornamenting the townscape.

Small areas of lawn, however pretty they may appear, should not be used in places or in sizes which will result in their overuse and ultimate degradation. No amount of careful maintenance or an abundance of 'keep off the grass' notices will prevent the erosion of the surface of a badly sited lawn. A well-worn Persian rug may have the appearance of faded splendour, but an over used lawn has none of that charm. The small lawn must be left to the private garden or the semi-public space where tight controls can be exercised. The formal lawn in Oxbridge colleges where social pressure prevents overuse or the railed garden of the London square spring to mind as successful examples of the use of lawns in cities (Figure 5.23). Areas of mown grass in the city should be large enough to absorb the effects of probable use and be accompanied by adequate paths following pedestrian desire lines. The edging or trim between lawn and footpath is important from a decorative and practical viewpoint. The smooth area of the path for walking should be edged with several rows of cobbles or similar hazard invoking material which act as a visual and physical constraint: the lawn edge is then raised 5-10 cm above the level of the cobbles to facilitate mowing. The public lawn with flower beds served by adequate footpaths is for many citizens the feature they would most associate with the beautiful or decorative city.

Routes through soft landscape where emergency access is required can be constructed with slab units designed to support emergency vehicles while retaining grass cover. The firepath is constructed in pre-cast concrete slabs taking the form of a grid made up of concrete castellations and regularly spaced pockets of soil in which grass may be seeded. The slabs are self-draining and have 75 per cent of the surface area in grass. Slabs of this kind, while expensive, can also be used for car parking surfaces to reduce the area of macadam.

Ground cover is a more expensive flooring material than grass but once established it excludes all weeds and requires very little maintenance. As a flooring material it is most useful in those areas having difficult access for mowing and maintenance. Even in the British climate, however, ground cover requires the proximity of watering points. Bedded out plants on roundabouts are clearly attractive to both ratepayer and visitor but maintenance costs are high: ground cover in such locations is an ideal form of soft landscaping and, if attractively arranged, it can be an acceptable alternative to the traditional flower bed.

CONCLUSION

The floor is the aspect of the city which is immediately apparent to the pedestrian. It is felt beneath the foot, seen at close quarters, from it the rain splashes and the heat rises to greet the user: its design is therefore of great importance. The choice of flooring must be appropriate for its use and fulfil the primary functions of comfort. Fortunately in fulfilling these functions flooring materials, both hard and soft, can present interesting and highly decorative patterning. Other aesthetic and symbolic functions enhance the range of decorative possibilities open to the designer in his or her attempt to ornament the city.

LANDMARKS, SCULPTURE AND FURNITURE   6

INTRODUCTION

There are two main aspects of city ornament. The first is the design and ornamentation of the two dimensional planes enclosing the network of streets and squares. This aspect of city ornament has been considered in previous chapters. This chapter deals with the second aspect of city ornament; the design and use of three dimensional objects, both buildings, major civic monuments and the more utilitarian elements of street furniture. The first decorative category, city spaces, falls within Lynch's definition of path and node. The second category, major three-dimensional objects within civic space fits most appropriately the definition of city landmark (Lynch, 1960). The distinction between these particular decorative elements is not exclusive and the boundary between typologies is not precise. For example, landmarks can take the form of a distinctive treatment of a wall surface, where two surfaces meet at a corner or where the roofline of a street elevation terminates in a distinctive and dramatic fashion. Conversely, city paths and nodes are frequently enriched with three dimensional objects, some of which act as landmarks.

There are two types of landmark. There is the purely local landmark which is visible from restricted locations. These are the points of reference by which we give directions to strangers in the locality. They are the 'innumerable signs, store fronts, door-knobs, and other urban detail, which fill the image of most observers' (Lynch, 1960). Without this rich array of local detail the urban scene would be greatly impoverished. The second type of landmark has city-wide relevance: it is a major point of reference shared by a large population. All landmarks share similar qualities. Unlike the street or square the observer does not enter into a landmark; they are external and usually a simply defined three dimensional object, a tower, dome or hilltop. Perceptually the form of a landmark is such that it is possible to single it out as an element or group of coherent elements against a background landscape of repetitive detail. The city-wide landmark is typically seen from a distance and from many angles, usually over the tops of or between lesser buildings. Both landmark types are important in creating a stimulating image for the observer and in assisting with the reading and understanding of the urban realm. In addition to these practical reasons for landmarks, they have an important role

Figure 6.1 The Castle
Rock, Nottingham

in creating a memorable urban landscape. The use of the landmark offers to the designer an opportunity to embellish the city with an intricate system of civic ornament. It is the landmark's decorative role in building the image of a place that is the chief concern of this chapter.

TYPOLOGY OF LANDMARKS

In physical terms there are two broad categories of landmarks: those that are natural - trees, hills and cliffs - and those that are constructed as part of the built environment. The second category of landmark divides quite naturally into buildings or parts of buildings and non-buildings or civic furniture. Both sub-categories of landmark again divide. Buildings can be attached or detached. Civic furniture can be singular, one-off elements - such as a great piece of sculpture - or it can be repetitive - that is multiple elements such as distinctive street lighting or a particular style and type of sign associated with a town or city quarter.

NATURAL FEATURES AS DECORATIVE ELEMENTS
In the rural or natural landscape distinctly shaped features - rocky outcrops, the single large tree or the hillside reminiscent of a human form - act as landmarks and reference points for orientation. On the smaller more intimate scale, natural local features such as a spring, change of vegetation type, or pronounced variation in geological structure, may provide important clues for image building. More often such local landmarks show evidence of man's intervention in nature - a crossroads, ruined cottage or ancient stone circle. The city, a largely man-made landscape, while no longer structured by ancient countryside lore, nevertheless retains, in man's perceptual organization and image building, an element of an older system of orientation. The landmark is possibly the most important of these memories from the past. The street map, diagram of the underground or metro system may be essential

6.1

for efficient modern movement in the city, nevertheless, more ancient clues remain important for a satisfactory relationship with the environment. Where natural landmarks appear in the urban fabric they perform the task of relating man to his contemporary environment but, possibly more importantly, to his deep roots in history. Such features are rare and should be protected. Nottingham is privileged to possess a massive rocky outcrop on which sits an architecturally uninspired castle (Figure 6.1). The rock on which the castle stands is riddled with caves and dungeons; it has a long history of settlement associated with the now culverted River Leen. Because of its long association with Nottingham's growth and development, it remains an important symbol, a historic landmark in the life of the city. However, from a visual point of view, it is the castle which from a distance announces the presence of the rock below. The same effect is attained in other cities, castles in Prague and Budapest being prime examples (Figure 6.2). The rocky outcrop from which Edinburgh Castle springs is probably a better known example of a natural landmark. Visitors to the city of Edinburgh walk down Prince's Street fully prepared for the sight of the castle but perhaps unaware of its sheer dominance in the urban landscape. A further example of the natural landmark is the rock of Mont St Michel in France, though in this case, the landmark has been significantly transformed by man's building activities which have stretched and extended nature's rocky form.

Natural features which are used for local landmarks and by which we structure the immediate neighbourhood include rivers, trees, local open space and scrubland. A great loss to the urban environment has been the culverting of the many smaller streams that once ran through the landscape which has now been colonized for urban land uses. The process of culverting arose because of the heavy pollution of streams in urban areas. It may now be apposite to consider de-culverting and naturalizing some of the many lost rivers running beneath city streets in concrete channels. A procedure such as this would return to the environment some of its lost visual and perceptual richness. It would also assist in reversing the process whereby the wasteful run-off of surface water in cities lowers the water table, damages underground aquifers and adds to the volume and therefore the cost of sewage treatment.

Natural vegetation, because of its rarity in cities, is often important in the perceptual image of the resident, particularly for children and young teenagers. Even the most derelict of wasteland can be a treasured landmark. In Nottingham, the arboretum, a narrow sliver of nineteenth century parkland that meanders across the main arteries of the city as they progress northwards, is both a highly decorative feature and an important natural landmark. Another natural landmark is to be found in Bath: the great trees at the centre of the Circus may not have been part of Wood's design but it is the trees, not the fine Circus, which constitutes the landmark. Any proposal to remove the trees and restore the Circus

Figure 6.2 The Castle, Budapest

to its eighteenth-century magnificence would not only cause great public outcry but would result in the loss of a highly decorative landmark.

BUILDINGS AS DECORATIVE ELEMENTS

The most usual type of landmark is a building or the upper part of a building such as a dome or steeple. For the building to impress itself as a landmark upon the urban scene and therefore upon the eye of the beholder, it must dominate the surrounding built forms or contrast sharply with them. By virtue of their size and scale such landmarks are the principal decorative element of a city. Particular buildings often provide the memorable image by which some cities are recognized, for example: St Paul's, London; St Peter's, Rome, and the Opera House, Sydney (Figure 6.3). Such buildings are thus civic monuments, performing a decorative and functional role in the city rather than being merely decorative in themselves; they are the chief monuments in a city and by virtue of this quality, they also act as the main landmarks. The building as landmark, may however, be no more than merely decorative.

Figure 6.3 Sydney Opera House

Rainaldi's twin churches at the Piazza del Popolo, Rome, for example, are emphatically a gratuitous decoration. As Abercrombie (1914) pointed out: 'Churches are the last thing, ordinarily, to be produced in pairs, like china vases.' Few buildings in the past have had patrons of sufficient social, political or religious significance or influence to create such civic monuments. Consequently where such buildings occur, they are often representative or expressive of the prevailing political, economic or religious structure giving order to the city. Prior to the modern period and the massive expansion of urban scale, these great personal expressions of power also provided a vital visual counterpoint to the surrounding urban fabric, which was usually characterized by a greater degree of uniformity. Within this more commonplace townscape the great civic monuments became a beacon for those occupying or using the city. Despite the changes wrought upon the urban scene by modern developments, the great building from the past still retains its rightful place as both landmark and major civic ornament.

While some great buildings act as the main city landmarks, it is often the setting of such landmarks which determines their decorative effect, enhances civic display and strengthens the imageability of the city. There are two broad types of civic setting for the great building. The first is the vernacular or organic traditions of city building of which Camillo Sitte wrote (1901). The second is the grand civic design scheme of monumental proportions which was anathema to Camillo Sitte. In each of these traditions the building as landmark is related to two other important perceptual structuring elements, the node and path.

A full account of the design of the urban square has been given elsewhere (Moughtin, 1992). This chapter is concerned, however, only with the square as a setting for a building which is also a major urban landmark. Zucker (1959) identified the relationship of such a monumental building and its associated urban space as an archetypal form which he categorized as the 'dominated square'. The dominated square is categorized by one individual structure or a group of buildings towards which the open space is directed and to which all other surrounding structures are related. This dominating building may be a church, palace, town hall, theatre or railway station. Sitte's analysis of urban space included two categories of piazza, similar to the dominated square of Zucker. Sitte (1901) distinguished two types of square, the 'deep' and the 'wide'. Both types were dominated by one building the proportions of which were reflected in the shape of the space: a tall church, for example, would be faced by a deep space receding from the façade while a long palace would be fronted by a long wide space of similar proportions to the main palace façade. The network of narrow picturesque streets of Sitte's ideal urban scene would enter the square at informal but concealed angles, from whence the viewer would be immediately aware of the imposing main building. It is on this building that most of the rich decoration was bestowed. A similar effect is achieved in more formal civic groupings. Often, as with Mansard's great palace in Versailles, the direction of the main street which opens into the square establishes the axis towards the dominant building. As Zucker (1959) notes, the apparent suction of the dominant structure and the perspective of the surrounding buildings create the spatial tension of the square, compelling the viewer to move towards and to concentrate on the focal architecture. The ornament concentrated on the façade of the main building reinforces this concentration of attention, fully establishing the landmark in the minds of both citizen and visitor.

The landmark that serves the city as a whole and even on occasions the surrounding region dominates the whole skyline. For example, the great cathedral at Lincoln, sited at the highest point in the city, dominates not only the surrounding urban area but also imposes itself upon the surrounding landscape. An account of the importance of skyline for city decoration has been outlined in Chapter 4. For the purpose of this discussion it is worth repeating that the building as landmark impinges upon the skyline and in turn decorates it with a profile that contrasts in size, scale and form with the surrounding structures. In Istanbul mosques not only decorate the skyline but also act as landmarks. The Blue Mosque with its six slender minarets encircling the dome which occupies a quarter of the space defined by them is an imposing monument occupying the centre of the Byzantium hippodrome. The same effect is achieved by the Fatih and Suleymaniye mosques while the Ortakoy mosque is a Rococo gem on the water's edge (Figure 6.4).

A building set at the head of a dominated square may or may not be detached from the surrounding buildings but if it is to be successful connections to flanking buildings must not distract from the landmark's dominance, distinction and apparent visual isolation. It must appear unique and quite separate from the surrounding buildings. The next section will concentrate upon those landmarks which are woven into the fabric of other buildings. Such buildings, or parts of buildings, are frequently

Figure 6.4 Ortakoy Mosque, Istanbul

only of a local significance but they are important for the richness and variety they give to the urban environment. They provide an opportunity for embellishment and fanciful decorative treatment.

The local landmark is usually associated with the network of paths that structure the city image. The street corner, where two paths meet and possibly where a node of social or economic activity has formed, is an obvious place for the development of a landmark. The form of the street corner has been discussed in Chapter 3: it is therefore sufficient here to emphasize that the forms of street corner most likely to lend themselves to the creation of a landmark are those of visually distinctive shape. For this purpose the towered corner with its break in the roofline results in a form which is clearly distinguished from its neighbours. If, in addition, the architectural treatment of the corner is highly ornamental and quite distinct from adjacent walls then the image produced is one which impinges upon the eye and the mind of the viewer. Corner types which merge into the background architecture, such as the curved corner, or those that make no positive visual statement, such as the angular corner, do not lend themselves to the type of distinctive decorative treatment necessary for the development of a landmark. The sweeping movement of the tower, piercing the roofline, is the corner type most predisposed to landmark formation. For greatest effect, however, it must be used with care and reserved for special locations.

Developers and architects appear to have rediscovered the street corner. Many recent urban developments celebrate the building corner with a flourish of decoration - the very antithesis of the multitude of neat but characterless acute angles that epitomize the more faceless examples of urban architecture of the 1950s and 1960s. While the new found interest in ornament is to be welcomed, if reproduced at every street corner such exuberance may result in a florid city-scape with no place for the eye to rest and the mind to recover. The overuse of the decorative street corner may in fact reduce its impact in the locations where a landmark is most essential. Where then should the highly decorative corner be used? Alexander (1987) suggests that paths should be articulated at 300 m intervals with a node. This node would seem a reasonable location for a landmark, particularly if it marks the meeting place of two or more important paths. It is important for the main network of paths to be modulated in this way to give interest and to provide the necessary structuring clues for navigation. It would also seem inappropriate for decorative corners of landmark status to be placed closer than three or four streets apart. At a distance of approximately 100-300 m along each main street or pathway there is an opportunity to introduce the towered corner as a landmark feature. The

remaining street corners would then take on the less decorative forms of the remaining types of external angles, not without decoration but subdued for the benefit of clarity and the creation of a strong city image.

NON-BUILDINGS AS DECORATIVE ELEMENTS

On a smaller scale, there are also autonomous three dimensional decorative elements, such as obelisks, fountains and sculpture, which decorate the city. Some of these features are either large or distinctive enough to act as landmarks. Examples in Nottingham are the lions in front of the Council House or the water clock in the Victoria Centre both of which act as meeting places for the teenager and therefore constitute important features of this group's mental map of the city.

In the second category of his typology, Zucker (1959) noted that the placement of a monument can be sufficiently strong in its impact to create around it a significant place in its own right. His archetype of a nuclear square relates to an urban space which is given coherence by the 'magnetism' of its monument. Although this spatial type is the most complex concept in his typology, Zucker notes that the aesthetic sensation of what he terms the nuclear square is no less real than the self-contained space of the enclosed or the dominated square. There is the impression of a distinct space. The perception of this space is critically reliant upon a nucleus, a strong vertical accent such as a monument, a fountain, obelisk or, as in the Place de l'Etoile, Paris, a triumphal arch, which is powerful enough to organize the space around it. This vertical accent ties the heterogeneous elements of the periphery into a single visual unit. As Zucker (1959) notes, this spatial unity is not endangered by any irregularity of the general layout or the haphazard position, size or shape of adjacent buildings: the sole determining factor in the perception of the space is the power, size and scale of the central monument. If the square in relation to the size of the focal monument becomes too large then the square loses its unity. An example of a space too large for its focal monument is Trafalgar Square which is too large and amorphous for Nelson's Column to act as a strong unifying nucleus.

Few autonomous monuments have sufficient presence to create significant urban spaces about them. Most civic furniture acts in harmony with or enhances by counterpoint the streets and squares of the city. Some major pieces of civic furniture may acquire the status of landmark but all, without exception, are used to decorate the city. An important aspect of urban design is to decorate the main urban spaces with appropriate ornaments: urban design is in part the art of furnishing the city and as previously suggested, all development should be judged as an attempt to decorate the city. Some furnishing, such as sculpture or fountains, may be purely decorative, others such as street lighting and seating may also have an important practical function. The emphasis in the following paragraphs is on such decorative elements as general, physical types: it is concerned with their properties and placement, rather than their detailed design.

THE GEOMETRIC PLACEMENT OF CIVIC MONUMENTS

In highly geometric or monumental civic design schemes autonomous three dimensional elements were employed to articulate, punctuate and accent the overall design. Their locations were principally determined by the geometric properties of the layout, particularly the primacy of, and symmetry about, the main axis of the composition. As Morris (1972) notes, throughout the Renaissance and the Baroque several dominant design considerations determined general attitudes to urbanization in all those countries affected by it. There was a preoccupation with: (i) symmetry of design elements to make a balanced composition about one or more axial lines; (ii) the closing of vistas by the careful placing of monumental buildings, obelisks or

suitably imposing statues, at the ends of long, straight streets; and (iii) individual buildings integrated into a single, coherent, architectural ensemble, frequently through the repetition of a basic elevational design.

Given the formality of the design in monumental schemes, there appears an inevitable location for any civic monument. The erection of the Obelisk in the Piazza del Popolo in 1589 is an example of this inevitability. The Obelisk was located after the planning of the third of the three radial roads into the square. The angle of this third and 'new' road, the Via del Babuino, was deliberately aligned with the pre-existing Via di Ripetta and Via Flaminia in order to form a focal point. On this focal point the Obelisk was raised. That the actual angles of the other streets are not precisely symmetrical about the Via Flaminia is demonstrated by the design of Rainaldi's two ostensibly identical churches, one of which has a circular plan, the other an elliptical plan. Both are placed in the angles between the streets. In this scheme the apparent inevitability of the location of the Obelisk is maintained despite the contingencies of the site.

Frequently, however, the apparent geometric inevitability of monumental layout has had its origins in the placement of the civic monument itself. It was often the siting of the monument which acted as the stimulus for the 'inevitable' layout that was the result. For example, Pope Sixtus V placed four obelisks in Rome between 1585 and 1590: in what was to became the Piazza del Popolo; on the Strada Felice immediately north-west of Santa Maria Maggiore; in front of San Giovanni in Laterano, and most significantly in front of the then unfinished St Peter's. The obelisk in the Piazza di San Pietro had therefore been placed before Bernini's great plan for the forecourt to the Cathedral (built in 1655-67). In preparing his layout, Bernini had to incorporate the central obelisk erected in 1586 by Pope Sixtus V and also the fountain constructed by Maderna in 1613 (Morris, 1972). It could be argued that Bernini bestowed on

Figure 6.5 The Grand
Arch, Paris

these two civic monuments a kind of post-rational-
ized inevitability. As Morris states, Pope Sixtus V had
very limited time in which to develop his plan for
Rome. The obelisks required a great effort to raise
and they were, nevertheless, effective tools in
concretizing his intention (Bacon, 1975). They established a critical mass of development which successive urban designers were reluctant or unable to
ignore. The location of the monuments established
the inevitability of the total layout. Such a sequence
of events illustrates Bacon's principle of the second
man: 'It is the second man who determines whether
the creation of the first man will be carried forward
or destroyed.'

Formal monumental schemes, if they are to be
human in scale, should not include axial vistas of
more than 1500 m. At this extreme distance the

'stopping of the axis' requires a monument of huge
bulk. A monument on the scale of the Arc de
Triomphe in Paris is necessary to terminate the
boulevards radiating from it successfully. It is more
usual for vistas of these dimensions to terminate
with a building such as the Grand Arch, Paris
(Figure 6.5). All of the buildings like the Arc de
Triomphe function as important and highly decorative visual cues or landmarks in the city structure.
However, following Alexander's suggestion that
nodes be placed at 300 m intervals along a path, the
long vista of 1500 m would require a series of minor
visual events, high points of both activity and
decorative interest, interspersing its length. It is this
richness of local interest that is sometimes lacking
in the monumental layout.

THE ORGANIC PLACEMENT OF CIVIC MONUMENTS

Alongside the tradition where three dimensional
decorative elements have been used to enrich the
overall monumental city design, the organic or
natural location of such elements has often been no
less deliberate and subtle. Guided, as Camillo Sitte
observed, according to artistic principles:

> Quite incomprehensible choices of location were
> made, and yet one must grant that a fine sensibility
> guided that choice since, as in the case of
> Michelangelo's David, everything always harmonised
> beautifully. Thus we are presented with a mystery –
> the mystery of the innate, instinctive aesthetic sense
> that worked such obvious wonders for the old
> masters without resort to narrow aesthetic dogma
> or stuffy rules. We, on the other hand, come along
> afterwards, scurrying about with T-square and
> compass, presuming to solve with clumsy geometry
> those fine points that are matter of pure sensitivity
> (Collins and Collins, 1986).

Sitte recommended that the location of fountains
and other foci of interest should not be

geometrically determined: they should be the result of an artistic activity guided by the invisible hand of creative sensibility.

Adshead, writing in the early decades of this century, appeared to be generally in agreement with the ideas of Sitte rejecting all notions of formal prescriptions for the siting of the main public monuments: 'To lay down hard-and-fast rules and regulations for the placing of statuary in towns would be to clip the wings of the imagination in its most fanciful flights; but to assume that principles cannot be hinted at which would be a guide to its arrangement and distribution would be a weakness amounting to the resignation of the intelligent criticism to the fickle antics of caprice' (Adshead, 1912d).

Sitte, however, was not averse to the examination of successful grouping of organically located monuments in the expectation of deriving a set of general principles to guide the urban designer, devoting a chapter of his book to the topic. For example, he derived a general principle for the placement of monuments, citing the analogy of children building snowmen, noting that they did not build them on the routes through the snow and likened those paths to routes crossing a square: 'Imagine the open square of a small market town in the country covered in deep snow and crisscrossed by several roads and paths that, shaped by the traffic, form the natural lines of communication. Between them are left irregularly distributed patches untouched by traffic. . . . On exactly such spots, undisturbed by the flow of vehicles, rose the fountains and monuments of old communities' (Collins and Collins, 1986). Sitte supported this notion, by pointing out that, as shown in old views and sketches of medieval and Renaissance cities, piazzas were mostly unpaved and the ground rarely levelled. This lead Sitte to speculate that when, for example, a fountain was to be installed it would not be set in the midst of the deep ruts left by wheeled vehicles, but on any of the undisturbed islands lying between the lines of communication. Later as the community grew larger and richer, the square may be graded and paved but the fountain would often remain where it stood. Even if the fountain were itself replaced at a later date, the new fountain was likely to remain at the same location.

One of the best examples of the organic location of a civic monument is the equestrian statue of the *Gattamaleta* by Donatello in front of S. Antonio in Padua, Italy. As Sitte states:

> Its remarkable, totally unmodern position cannot be recommended too highly for study. At first one is struck by its gross offence against today's invariable and solely acceptable manner of placement. Then one notices the admirable effect of the monument at this unusual spot, and, in the end, it becomes clear that if the monument were placed in the centre of the plaza the effect would not be nearly as great. Once the move away from the centre is accepted, all the rest follows naturally, including in this case the orientation of the statue in relation to the entering streets (Collins and Collins, 1986).

One of the finest and most sensitive examples of the organic and piecemeal accumulation of statuary is to be found in the Piazza della Signoria in Florence. Here the statues and monuments assist the eye in forming two interpenetrating spaces from the 'L' shaped Piazza:

> The main square forms two distinct, but interpenetrating, spaces their boundary being defined by an optical barrier of sculpture; Michelangelo's David, Bandinelli's Hercules and Cacus group, Donatello's Judith, Ammanati's large Neptune fountain and the equestrian statue of Cosimo Medici by Giovanni da Bologna. Using this device a formless, medieval space was converted into two spaces with proportions corresponding more closely to Renaissance ideals. The process was started in 1504, with the placing of Michelangelo's David to the left of the palace entrance, a decision given great thought by many experts. The line of sculpture was completed in 1594 by the placing of the equestrian statue at the centre point of the imaginary border line of both squares. The line of statues parallel to the east

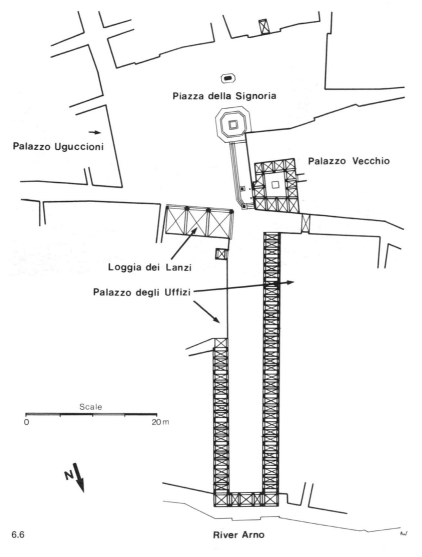

Piazza della Signoria

Palazzo Uguccioni

Palazzo Vecchio

Loggia dei Lanzi

Palazzo degli Uffizi

Scale

0   20 m

N

River Arno

6.6

6.7

Figure 6.6 Plan of Piazza della Signoria, Florence
Figure 6.7 Piazza della Signoria, Florence

façade of the Palazzo Vecchio, continues to the dome of the cathedral, while the subtle placing of the Neptune fountain, at forty-five degrees to the corner of the palace acts as a fulcrum about which both spaces pivot (Sitte, 1901) (Figures 6.6 and 6.7).

Sitte's views on the placement of statues, monuments and fountains were a reaction to the leaden neo-baroque and academic formalism prevailing during his time. The result of such formalism was a stultifying insistence on axial planning and long vistas. Sitte claimed that the impulse to centre something perfectly in a square is an 'affliction' of modern times. Nevertheless, Christopher Alexander (1977) makes an analogy with a table: 'Imagine a bare table in your house. Think of the power of the instinct which tells you to put a candle or a bowl of flowers in the middle. And think of the power of the effect once you have done it. Obviously, it is an act of great significance; yet clearly, it has nothing to do with activities at the edge or in the centre.' Alexander, however, concedes that the effect may be purely formalistic 'the sheer fact that the space of the table is given a centre, and the point at the centre then organises the space around it, and makes it clear and puts it roughly at rest. The same thing happens in a courtyard or a public square.' Nevertheless Alexander's prescriptive pattern remains essentially true to Sitte's view: 'Between the natural paths which cross a public square or court-yard or a piece of common land choose something to stand roughly in the middle: a fountain, a tree, a statue, a clock-tower with seats, a windmill, a bandstand. Make it something which gives a strong and steady pulse to the square, drawing people in toward the centre. Leave it exactly where it falls between the paths; resist the impulse to put it exactly in the middle.'

Elbert Peets (1927), in his review of Sitte's work, qualifies his outright condemnation of the centring of public monuments in public places and along axial lines in formal compositions. Peets thought that Sitte's preference for the picturesque qualities of the urban landscape caused him to fail to appre-ciate the reasons for such placements during the Renaissance. According to Peets, Renaissance designers set fountains and monuments on the axes of buildings in order that, by the optical law of parallax, the spectator might have the means of measuring his distance from the building he was approaching and thus have a lively impression of the extent of the area and the size of the building. Peets does, however, agree with Sitte's view that the centre of a building or any other particularly decorative part of a building should not be obstructed by a monument. Not only, according to Peets, would such monuments obstruct a richly articulated section of the building, but such decora-tion would be a poor and confusing background for a finely modelled ornament.

Before considering the particular siting require-ments of a range of civic monuments it is appropri-ate to summarize the general principles of their organic placement as outlined by Sitte and modified by his followers. The first principle is the need for a neutral background for the monument: 'The decisive difference in this case between the past and present

is that we always look for places as magnificent as possible for every little statue, thus diminishing its effect instead of augmenting it, as could be done by means of the neutral background that a portraitist would choose for his heads under the circum-stances' (Collins and Collins, 1986). The second principle is that monuments should be placed in areas that do not conflict with traffic movement: 'To the ancient rule of placing monuments around the edge of public squares is thus allied another that is genuinely medieval and more northern in character: to place monuments and especially market fountains at points in the square untouched by traffic' (Collins and Collins, 1986). The third principle, and the one where there is some ambivalence from later writers, is that the centre of the square should be kept free for activities associated with the square. Perhaps this principle can be tempered by the suggestion that in some spaces the centre is the inevitable position for a statue or monument. The best example is, of course, the location of the equestrian statue of Marcus Aurelius in the Campidoglio, Rome. Other well known examples include the statue of Stanislas

Figure 6.8 Equestrian statue, Piazza SS Annunziata, Florence

Figure 6.9 Arch of Constantine, Rome

in Place Stanislas, Nancy and the equestrian statue of the Grand Duke Ferdinand on the axis of the Church of Santissima Annunziata in the Piazza Della Santissima Annunziata, Florence (Figure 6.8). Perhaps less well known is the monument at the centre of the main square in Villa Real, Portugal. Here the insistent pattern of the floor draws the eye to the centre and the vertical column which strengthens the spatial composition of the square in the same fashion as the equestrian statue in the Campidoglio.

CIVIC MONUMENTS AS DECORATIVE ELEMENTS

In the Town Planning Review between 1911 and 1915, S. D. Adshead wrote a series of articles on the decoration and furnishing of the city. Adshead dealt with what he called 'non-utilitarian furnishings with which we embellish our Parks and Towns', for

example monumental arches, fountains and clocks. In addition he also dealt with features 'which essentially utilitarian in their purpose, if well designed and carefully placed can add enormously to the stateliness and beauty of the street.' These were utilitarian furnishings such as lamp standards, tall lighting standards, masts and flag poles, shelters, refuges and protection posts, and trees. Many of these were a result of the more widespread appearance in cities of that period of motor cars and other motorized transport.

THE MONUMENTAL ARCH

There are three main types of monumental arch. The most well known is the Triumphal Arch which is of mainly Roman origin, though there are similar features in trabeated form dating back to the cities of Pharaonic Egypt. Second there is the arch used as a portal: its main function however, has often been a defensive structure in the city wall. Another tradition in Europe for this feature of city architecture is the walled cities of medieval times. The third and final monumental arch is the temporary structure erected to celebrate a particular event.

The 'Arc de Triomphe' as a feature of the European city, has its origin of form and placement in the world of Ancient Rome (Figure 6.9). The reasons for its erection were as a symbol commemorating conquest, colonization and victory at war. It was also used to commemorate great engineering or architectural feats. The arch used for any of these purposes was usually placed at the termination of an avenue or important path, on the crown of a hill, a meeting place or node, and at the entrance to some great architectural or engineering construction such as a bridge.

Adshead (1911a) states that the Roman monumental arch was regarded as a pedestal for statuary and sculpted reliefs. The earliest monumental arch had one opening and was later developed to the now familiar form of a large central arch flanked by two smaller subsidiary arches. The form of the triumphal pedestal with single arch is best

6.10

6.11

Figure 6.10 Marble Arch, London
Figure 6.11 City gateway, York

displayed by the one built in memory of Trajan at Ancona to celebrate the restoration of the harbour. Good examples of the three-arched triumphal pedestal are Constantine's Arch and the Arch of Septimus Severus both in Rome. By far the greater number of Roman triumphal pedestals consisted of one central arch with most of the rest of the surface decorated with sculptured bas-reliefs. The top of the pedestal was surmounted by statuary and memorabilia usually from wartime exploits. The whole triumphal arch would have been used to record a particular account of a historical event which had provided an opportunity to decorate the city with an imposing monument. One of the best known more recent examples in the Roman triumphal arch tradition is the Arc de Triomphe in Paris, erected at Place de l'Etoile to commemorate the victories of Napoleon. In Britain the triumphal arch is best

represented by the one on Constitution Hill by Decimus Burton and by the Marble Arch both in London (Figure 6.10). The All-India War Memorial by Lutyens for New Delhi is in the tradition of Rome and its placement on the main axis of the plan for the city follows the usual pattern of location for such monuments.

Medieval Europe was rich in examples of city gateways (Figure 6.11). The prime function of such arched openings in city walls was one of control, mainly for defence but often for the protection of the city market and its commercial interests. The arched opening in the medieval city did have other functions of an aesthetic origin: it did for example, symbolize the entrance or city threshold and thus the city itself. The origins of this celebration of the threshold can be traced to Hellenic Greece and to Greece during Mycenaean times. The propylaea at

Figure 6.12 The Charminar, Hyderabad, India

Figure 6.13 Triumphal Arch, Nancy

6.12

6.13

Tyrins may indeed have foreshadowed its much later and more famous Propylaea designed by Mnesicles for the Acropolis in Athens: this is the model, though trabeated, for all city gateways. To see the decorative function of the portal fully developed in medieval times it is necessary to turn to the great Islamic cities where the portal announced the presence of the city, cemetery and mosque, or as in Hyderabad, India identified the location of the city centre (Figure 6.12).

France, during the Renaissance, saw the merger of the Roman triumphal arch tradition with the medieval concept of the city gateway or portal. For example, some fine portals were built as gateways to Paris, including Porte Saint-Martin and Porte Saint-Denis. Outside Paris many fine gateways were built in provincial capitals. For example, Nancy is endowed with Porte des Illes, Porte Stanislas, Porte Saint-Nicolas and Porte Sainte-Catherine (Figure 6.13). In Britain during the nineteenth century this tradition was continued with many fine monumental arches completed. One of the best examples to be found is the portal to Birkenhead Park, the Wirral.

The last type of arch used in the decoration of the city is the temporary arch. The tradition of the temporary decorative arch goes back many centuries: for example, Napoleon commissioned such an arch to celebrate his marriage to Josephine. Designed by Percier and Fontaine in the Imperial Style, it is said by Adshead (1911a) to have been one of the most beautiful of street decorations ever conceived. Belfast still holds to this tradition of city decoration using temporary arches to adorn Protestant streets during the 'marching season' in July. Despite the overtones of chauvinism such features, nevertheless, celebrate a community's spirit and by their colourful spontaneity add a decorative dimension to a city in need of a human touch.

This century has seen the destruction of many fine city gateways to make way for the encroaching motor car. In towns like Kings Lynn the original settings of the gateways have been destroyed to permit the car to pass unhindered. With current

Figure 6.14 Place Vendôme, Paris

attitudes to pedestrianizing large areas of the city centre, particularly in continental Europe, the portal could again become an important feature in the urban structure of the city.

MONUMENTAL COLUMNS

There are two main types of monumental columns. The first has its origins in Hellenic and Hellenistic Greece while the second type is associated with Ancient Rome and is the development of the Greek column on an altogether grander scale. Pliny, writing in approximately AD 50, explains that statues of great men are placed on columns to raise them above statues of ordinary men (Adshead, 1911b). He was also of the opinion that the custom of erecting monumental columns for statues was a much older tradition than that of building triumphal arches. Since the idea of the monumental column is Greek in origin and the triumphal arch, as such, was never used in Hellenic cities, this may in fact be the case.

The Greek monumental pedestal or column was small in scale, consisting of a highly decorative shaft, fluted and carved with acanthus leaves or twisted serpents. The top of the shaft was reserved for an allegorical figure or symbol, for example at Olympia it was the winged figure of Victory, while at Delphi it was a group of Caryatid Dancers or an archaic Sphinx. The monumental column shaft of the early Greek period was not based upon a typical column from the temple; it was an appropriately designed pedestal for the specific purpose of supporting a fine piece of sculpture which was to be seen and appreciated from the ground.

6.15

6.16

Figure 6.15 Nelson's Column, Trafalgar Square, London
Figure 6.16 Detail of base, Wren's Column, London, illustrating its vast scale

Trajan's Column is probably the most notable of the monumental columns erected by the Romans. According to Adshead (1911b): 'A particularly beautiful feature of this column is the festoon of bay leaves which is wreathed around its pedestal, and upon which rest four eagles at the corners.' The siting of the column in a small enclosed courtyard off the main Basilica of Trajan increased the dramatic effect of this highly decorative column. Columns similar in form to that of the Trajan Column were erected in cities throughout the Roman Empire though most have been destroyed or have disappeared.

Important columns of the Roman monumental type have been erected in European cities until comparatively modern times. Of these the Doric column designed by a pupil of Blondel for Place Vendôme, Paris, is an outstanding example erected in 1810 to commemorate victories by Napoleon (Figure 6.14). Similar columns for the Duke of Wellington were erected at the southern end of Nash's composition for Regent Street, London and a particularly fine example was located in Liverpool amongst the great civic buildings of the nineteenth century. Nelson's Column in Trafalgar Square, London is another column of this type, a particularly popular decorative feature of the city for Londoners (Figure 6.15). Possibly the finest column in Britain, however, is the great Doric shaft designed by Wren in about 1671 to commemorate the Fire of London. Though badly sited, its elegant detailing and sheer size, 174 ft (53 m) as against Trajan's column at 115 ft (35 m) or the Vendôme column at 116 ft (35.5 m), establishes the preeminence of this monument (Figure 6.16).

In addition to using monumental columns the Romans adorned public places with columns of a smaller type. The Rostral Column is closer to the tradition of the Greek monumental column and closer to a scale which would be acceptable today. The unadorned severity of some of the more gigantic of the Roman type columns which appeared in European cities in the last century diminished their power as aesthetic decorative statements. It was not until the neo-Greek revival that the monumental column took on new possibilities with a greater freedom of decorative treatment, when the column shaft was fluted, banded, rusticated and festooned with garlands repeating a style common to Hellenic Greece. Columns and pedestals of small scale are more adaptable for the smaller public spaces and suitable to commemorate the lives of mere mortals, the scientists, teachers and clerics rather than the heroic figures of the semi-deity. Many fine examples of small scale pedestals ornament the town squares of countries like Portugal and Spain celebrating the useful lives of valued citizens.

OBELISKS

The origin of the obelisk is undoubtedly Egyptian. Its popularity as a special decorative element in the city is attested by the way in which other peoples have, from time to time, raided Egypt for this particular treasure. More than forty Egyptian obelisks have survived though few remain in their original location: twelve were transported to Rome, five to Britain, one to New York, one to Paris and several are in Istanbul. The form of the obelisk has been copied for its use in many towns and villages in Britain and in mainland Europe (Figure 6.17). Only the smaller of these copies however, use the monolith in true Egyptian style which is made of a single piece of stone.

The obelisk with its vertical emphasis has no horizontal directional quality, it can therefore be used to mark the centre of an axis or the crossing point of two or more axes. It does not however form a stop or point of termination to a vista. The

Figure 6.17 Obelisk, Southport

obelisk, as in St Peter's Square, Rome and in the Place de la Concorde, Paris, can be made to form the hub of a great place. Unlike the monumental column which frequently stands alone, the obelisk is used to support a larger conception or design. Probably the most notable example of the use of the obelisk in city planning is the work carried out by the architect Domenico Fontana under the instructions of Pope Sixtus V. Between the years 1585 and 1590 the medieval city of Rome was transformed. The technique Pope Sixtus V used to create order out of the chaos of the medieval city was the long vista. Using wide, straight roads he connected the seven main churches, the holy shrines which had to be visited by pilgrims in the course of the day. Incorporating the work of previous Popes he developed a whole new communication network of major access routes through the city (Figure 6.18). At the termination of his great vistas, in this communication network, obelisks were raised and around these, and other important nodes along the route, squares were later to develop. As Rasmussen (1969) states: 'In this way, the obelisks became gigantic

Figure 6.18 Plan of Rome
by Pope Sixtus V

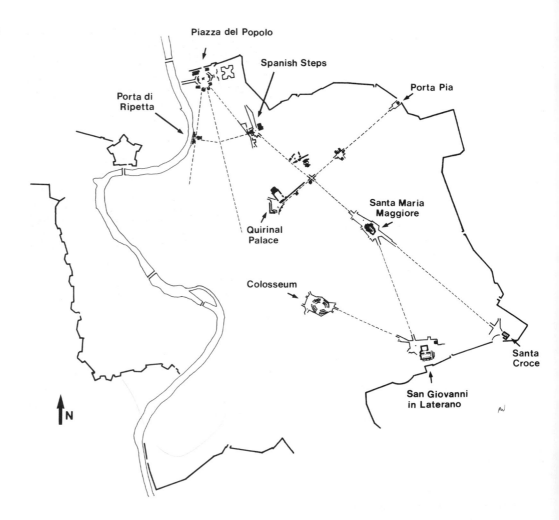

surveyor's rods marking out a system of straight lines, the plan of the future.'

Rasmussen, however, misses the point when he dismisses the raising of the obelisks as having no symbolic meaning: 'For the Egyptians they had been a part of a religious cult, for the ancient Romans a symbol of world dominion, but for the Popes and their architects they had no symbolic meaning whatsoever, only an artistic one'. Adshead (1911c)

more perceptively suggests that the obelisk 'should be set up only as marking the commencement of a new era in national events'. The rebuilding of Rome after its fall and subsequent decline in the Middle Ages, was such a national event of major significance. The city planning of Sixtus V was not simply concerned with the building of great religious processional routes; he was a practical man and part of his development plan was to bring water to the higher and under-utilized parts of the city, a daring feat requiring great engineering skills. Part of the plan was to open up for development new tracts of land previously unoccupied. Since obelisks are 'the most appropriate of all monuments to typify perpetuity and endurance' (Adshead, 1911c), their use epitomized the vision displayed by Sixtus V in his master plan for the regeneration of Rome.

DECORATIVE CLOCKS

The town clock is an object with a propensity for registering a strong impression on the eye and the mind of the passer-by. The clock, if carefully sited and with sensitively designed setting, is a potential landmark with a strong visual image. One of the great landmarks of London is Big Ben, its chime being as important as its appearance for the function of landmark: its chime is as decorative as the tower in which the clock is housed. Clocks, however, do not need to be on the scale of Big Ben to register as important decorative city elements. For example, clocks and accompanying bells in Prague, Munich and St Mark's in Venice, though small, bring great charm to the urban scene (Figure 6.19). Public clocks are not only useful but are also attractive items of street furniture.

There are four types of decorative clock used to furnish the city: (i) the tower clock; (ii) the bracket clock; (iii) the monumental clock, and (iv) the post-mounted clock. As a replacement for the sundial, clocks were at first fixed on church towers. Later, towers erected for the specific purpose of receiving a clock were considered necessary for all public buildings. Traditionally they have been provided as a demonstration of prestige being placed on town halls, inns, hospitals, bus and railway stations in addition to church towers. The bracket clock cantilevered from the street façade is a highly ornamental piece of street furniture. Where the façade is flat and unmodelled it gives a point of interest for those walking on the pavement bringing life and vitality to the street scene. To achieve maximum impact the bracket clock should not be

Figure 6.19 Clock, Old Square, Prague

lost in a profusion of other hanging or cantilevered signs and advertisements. The clock monument is a development of the tower clock but it is an isolated feature standing freely in public space rather like the monumental column (Figure 6.20). Unlike the arch, obelisk and column, the clock monument has no hereditary form.

Adshead (1912a) writing at the beginning of this century, is scathing in his criticism of clock monuments of his period. However, clock monuments similar to those dismissed at the start of this century by Adshead if located in any city would now be protected as treasured possessions. It is, however, difficult to imagine similar monuments being constructed now. A simple structure such as

Figure 6.20 Clock
monument, Newmarket
Figure 6.21 Fountain,
Castle Howard, Yorkshire

6.20

6.21

the post-mounted clock based upon the street lighting standard, 'high tech' concept or playful ornate sculpture, such as the musical clock in Nottingham's Victoria Centre, are more likely sources of ideas for the clock monument of today.

WATER IN THE CITY

Water has an elemental quality which gives it great symbolic meaning when used as a decorative feature in the city. Water together with trees and the canopy of the sky above reminds us of the wildness of nature. Water in the city links the citizen to his or her deep roots to mountain range, spring, gurgling brook, deep chasm and mighty waterfall. Since the origin of cities, man has used water not only for essential purposes but also for display. The bringing of water to the city was often a great undertaking, involving the building of a giant aqueduct, or the digging of vast systems of canals, using an immense labour force.

Water is an essential attribute to every urban landscape. Few cities can claim to be artistically embellished without the use of water in their streets, squares and parks. Ancient Rome was a city of fountains while villas in and around Rome and Florence dating from the fifteenth and sixteenth centuries still captivate the visitor. There is no comparison between these models from history and our own meagre efforts this century. For example, Nottingham's two pools in front of the Council House are poor descendants of the fountains in the Villa D'Este outside Rome. Water can be used in a city to convey a number of different moods and impressions. It can be used as still pools, waterfalls, jets, fountains, bowls or with sculpture (Figure 6.21).

Quiet, still waters place a mirror before the city. Holland possesses some fine urban canalscapes where we see the actual city and its mirror image in the long still stretch of water. The quiet Moghul parks of northern India are a world apart from the bustling activity of nearby Srinagar, Kashmir: the gardens descend the easy slope from reflecting pool to reflecting pool, separated only by small tumbling falls; the lovely garden structures surrounded by and reflected in the pools add to the charm and serenity.

The turbulent gushing qualities of the great waterfall are captured in the water garden of Villa d'Este. The frenetic activity of the fountains, jets and cascading water recreates the sense of visual and aural turmoil of nature's finest waterfalls. The visual quality of water depends upon its reflection of light. The droplets from falling water and the ripples they cause on the surface sparkle, while reflecting and refracting the light into a myriad of pinpoints of brilliance and colour. Also important to the visual quality of water are its sounds as it splashes and gurgles. These sounds, together with the spray and the pinpoints of bright, cold light, bestow upon water a special place in the hot polluted city - the quality of cooling is particularly welcome, civilizing and decorative. This is particularly true of moving water, whether it is the thunderous waterfall or the gently moving stream directed down the slope and agitated from side to side by a decorative sculpted channel. For pure visual excitement, however, no greater sight can be imagined than the great water jet capturing, as it soars 60-90 m, the power of nature's geyser. The city of Geneva attempts to capture this effect with a water jet in the lake decorating the central area.

Water in the street or square is not normally associated with the torrent and only in cities such as Venice or Amsterdam does water take on the function of large reflecting pool. The small still pool and larger-than-life water display are both normally reserved for green areas within or without the city boundaries. The fountain is probably the most appropriate water sculpture with which to decorate the street and square. The fountain has many forms and is therefore difficult to analyse in terms of design principles: 'fountains, which of all works of art that contribute to the furnishing and equipment of the fully-developed town, are most intangible and least amenable to the recognised laws of proportion,

Figure 6.22 Trevi Fountain, Rome

grammatical analysis, and the restrictions of style' (Adshead, 1912c). The fountain varies from the bowl, the simplest form of sculpture with water, to the great Baroque composition with figures, jets and falls, such as the Fontana di Trevi, erected by Clement II in 1735 from designs by Niccolo Salvi. The distinctive architectural form of the Trevi has given to the fountain a reputation that raises its profile to one that symbolizes Rome, a compulsory sight for all visitors, a landmark of truly international significance (Figure 6.22).

As Adshead (1912c) notes in placing a fountain, whatever form it may take, 'careful consideration should in the first instance be given to the contours of the site. The natural position for a fountain is not on the heights and plateaus of the park and of the city but in the cups, in the hollows and in the plains.' The fountain designed as a water jet is a translucent and diaphanous object and in the narrow confines of an urban scheme it is not appropriate as its pivot or centre. Adshead cautions that 'where surrounded by architecture the fountain is better designed primarily as an architectural feature

6.23

Figure 6.23 Fountain, Piazza del Commune, Assisi
Figure 6.24 Fountain, Piazza SS Annunziata, Florence

6.24

adorned with sculpture from which may gush forth water as falls or jets.' Good examples of this type of fountain are to be found in the Piazza Navona, Rome. The fountain, as Sitte (1901) points out, should not take a central position, it should be to one side as in many medieval cities. Particularly good examples can be seen in the Cathedral Square, Perugia, in the main square in Assisi and Piazza SS Annunziata, Florence (Figures 6.23 and 6.24). Adshead argues that something more tangible than a mere jet of water is needed as the pivot of an architectural group; the fountain should be a satellite to the more robust elements of the scheme. The importance of this principle is well illustrated in the Piazza Obliqua in front of St Peter's, Rome, in the Place de la Concorde, Paris, and in Trafalgar Square, London. Cabot Square in London's Canary Wharf contradicts this principle by placing the fountain at the centre of the square (Figure 6.25).

The simple bowl can lift water above eye level without resource to great pressures. The water can then tumble by gravity from bowl to bowl. The bowl itself is a lovely shape and can increase the feeling of water through noise and movement without great volumes of water or costly sculptural compositions. It is probably the bowl or combination of bowls with small fountain that is most appropriate for modern needs of water in the city street and square.

URBAN SCULPTURE

The use of statues for city decoration has a long and distinguished history. Despite this long history there are no infallible rules for the placing of statuary.

There are, however, some general principles to
guide the arrangement and distribution of sculpture
in cities. Being definitive about these principles has
been made more difficult by the social changes
which have occurred since the First World War. The
changes include public attitudes to art; rapid, almost
frenetic stylistic changes in art; changes in acceptable subject matter for public art; changes in architectural styles which omitted sculpture from its
design repertoire; and changes in materials and
construction methods for sculpture.

There are three main traditional types of statuary:
(i) the single figure, (ii) the group and (iii) the
equestrian statue. The single figure is problematic as
a decorative feature in the contemporary city. In the
Western world's age of democracy, it seems
inappropriate to decorate the city with heroic
figures of Gods, dictators or allegorical figures of
some sentimentalized mythical or jingoistic past.
Alternatively, placing a statue of a valued citizen
poses a problem of scale. Even a group of such
figures can look out of place. For example, the
group of figures in Market Square, Nottingham, is
totally lost and out of scale in the large arena of the
main city square (Figure 6.26). Placing the group in
a tub of daffodils does not assist a clumsy setting. A
similar group of figures placed in a much smaller
space behind Liverpool Street Station, London, is
much more successful (Figure 6.27). The informal
placing of statuary suggested by Sitte and outlined
earlier may be a useful guide for the placing of
small scale sculptures. The small scale pedestals for
busts and statues found in the squares of Portugal,
described earlier, may also be a useful model.

6.25

6.26

Figure 6.25 Fountain, Cabot Square, Canary Wharf,
London

Figure 6.26 Sculpture, Market Square, Nottingham

Figure 6.27 Sculpture, Broadgate, London
Figure 6.28 Sculpture, Bogota

6.27

6.28

The equestrian statue has a long pedigree. It is best placed commanding an expanse of open space. Where occupying favoured sites of this type they are seen to greatest advantage when placed on lofty pedestals. There are two particularly fine examples of equestrian statues dating from the Renaissance. They are the Colleoni by Verrochio for the Piazza di SS Giovanni e Paolo in Venice and its great rival the Gattamelata at Padua by Donatello. According to Zucker (1959), Verrocchio's equestrian sculpture is powerful enough to charge the space around with a tension that keeps the whole composition together, evoking the impression of a square despite the amorphous and disconnected building shapes which form the edge of a highly irregular shape.

There seem few, if any, opportunities, outside totalitarian states, for the use today of the colossus,

the great national monument such as the Statue of Liberty or the monumental statues of Christ in Rio and Lisbon. For example, the former Stalin Monument in Prague, once visible from almost every part of the city - a 30 m high granite sculpture portraying a procession of people being led to Communism by the Pied Piper figure of Stalin, popularly dubbed 'the bread queue' - provided identity for the city. In townscape and decorative terms, it made sense as the terminal feature of the vista along the Parizska leading from the Old Square. However, its symbolism of oppression and subjugation of the Czech people outweighed townscape considerations and it was dynamited in 1962 following Khrushchev's denouncement of his predecessor. The monument has been replaced by a metronome which does not have the same townscape qualities while the base has become a site for protest and graffiti. There are also few opportunities to celebrate the deeds of the national hero or heroine either on foot or on horse. The city sculpture which decorates the contemporary city is likely to be a shark protruding from a rooftop, or the nose of an aeroplane bursting through a façade or fanciful neon lights decorating the theatre front. Such decorative features of the city defy analysis and result from playful creativity (Figure 6.28).

UTILITARIAN STREET EQUIPMENT

The street furnishings so far discussed are necessary for the complete decoration of the city; like the fine pictures on the living room wall or flowers in the centre of the dining room table, their chief purpose is to delight. There is, however, some street equipment with a function that is primarily utilitarian. It could be argued that columns, clock towers and fountains also have a function, even if it is simply of a symbolic nature. It can also be argued that the bus shelter, street light and park bench, though functional, can be and should be well designed attractive street sculpture in purely formal terms.

An important purpose of all street equipment is to establish, support or strengthen the *genius loci* of a place. Pevsner (1955) wrote 'The genius of the place, the *genius loci*, is a mythological person taken over from antiquity and given a new meaning. The *genius loci*, if we put it in modern terms, is the character of the site, and the character of the site is, in a town, not only the geographical but also historical, social and especially the aesthetic character.' The choice of sets of compatible street furniture can give identity to a particular city, district in a city or institution of a city. For example, the entrances to

Figure 6.29 Metro, Paris

the Paris Metro are in a quite distinctive art nouveau style (Figure 6.29). Designed by Hector Guimard (1867-1942) they are highly evocative of Paris, possessing far more charm and identity than their utilitarian equivalents in other major cities. Similarly, the red telephone boxes in English villages designed by George Gilbert Scott, have made a significant contribution to the *genius loci* of the English rural scene (Figure 6.30). British Telecom's and Mercury's replacements, though functional have none of the character of the red telephone box. To a lesser extent, the art deco kiosks and fittings designed by Rowse for the entrances to the Mersey Tunnel performed the same function of 'identity'; in this case, however, it was the institution not Liverpool or Birkenhead which was identified.

According to Lynch's theories, the city with clearly identifiable and distinct districts lends itself to the creation of a strong perceptual image in the viewer. This strong visual image facilitates the user's

Figure 6.30 Telephone box, London
Figure 6.31 Arch, China Town, Soho, London

6.30

6.31

understanding of the city and therefore its management and use by the individual. An important question arises about the scope for, and desirability of, facilitating this process of district identification through the deliberate choice or design of distinct sets of street furniture for each district in the city. 'China Town' in London's Soho is an example where a policy of street furniture designed specifically for a given location appears to have been successful. The Chinese shops with signs in Chinese, the gateway and telephone kiosks, again in a Chinese style, give the place a unity and a successful decorative quality (Figure 6.31). Can the same be said for the Regency style fittings for London's Regent Street? Glancey (1992), for one, does not think so: 'There should be limits to the British obsession with heritage. When functional, workaday objects such as traffic lights, bus shelters and "No Entry" signs have to be dressed up in Regency fancy dress to keep us Quality Street-sweet, heritage has given way to idiocy. This is what has happened to

Regent Street, London, where a four million pound programme of public works by the Crown Commissioners, . . . has given us the world's first Regency traffic lights.' He regrets that the standard 'blackness' of street fittings associated with London was not used (Figure 6.32). 'If only the signs, lights etc were painted black - the traditional colour of London lampposts, railings and traffic lights - then at least the clutter of urban accessories would be subdued. The vile blue paintwork, however, clashes violently with the red of Regent Street's pillar boxes and buses, . . . the black of its taxis and the muted grey of its buildings and pavements.'

Most utilitarian street furniture is recent in origin with little if any historic precedent for design purposes. The eighteenth-century street would have been free from obstructions such as street furniture. The only exceptions would have been the occasional inn sign and local horse trough. Those utilitarian items, such as lampposts or bollards and chains, used occasionally to furnish the major civic

6.32

6.33

Figure 6.32 Street
furniture, Regent Street,
London
Figure 6.33 Street
furniture, Piazza of St
Mark's, Venice

spaces were few in number and well placed. The
ironwork screen used for the protection of privacy
or as an enclosure was carefully sited, as for
example, at the corners of Place Stanislas in Nancy.
In contrast to this orderly well placed street furniture, modern streets appear to be filled with a
clutter of signs, kiosks, lampposts of various size
and shape, overhead wires and advertisement hoardings. They are invariably placed with little consideration for their grouping and the effect they have on
the street scene. Bringing order out of this chaos is
a task of the urban designer. This is an aspect of
city design which is beginning to receive the attention it deserves. The prophetic remarks of Adshead
(1913d) are beginning to take effect: 'We are only

commencing to realise that the placing of town
furnishings both ornamental and useful can be made
a potent factor in adding dignity, formality, and
beauty to the public thoroughfare and "place".'

Adshead (1914a) later suggests that the Roman
Candelabra is a precursor of the lamp standard or
lamppost. This is probably true of the early lamp
standards of Adshead's period which were associated initially with gas lighting. It is by no means
true, however, of some of the simpler modern
examples of tapering steel post surmounted by a
globe. Such modern lampposts have more in
common with the three elegant poles in front of the
Basilica in the Piazza San Marco, Venice; close by in
the Piazzetta are some beautifully sculptural light

Figure 6.34 Gas lamp, Park Estate, Nottingham

standards which give a soft glow at night but lovely silhouette by day (Figure 6.33). Gas lighting in the streets of the Park Estate, Nottingham, recreates a dim Victorian gloom on long foggy winter evenings. It is fortunate to find here, in this conservation area, the original Victorian cast iron gas light standard still functioning as designed and still contributing to the overall unity in the Park (Figure 6.35). In other areas of historic interest, the Victorian lamppost has been adapted to or copied for use with electric street lighting with some success.

A city can often be judged by its benches, their location, number and comfort. The bench or group of benches is often the location of activity for different age groups. The bench is a civilizing influence in a city and most appropriately sited in its streets, squares and parks, particularly when the definition of civilization is taken to mean the culture of living in cities. The bench is a place for the old to sit in the sun to pass the time of day, for students to study, for the office worker to have lunch, for the young to embrace and for shoppers to rest their weary feet.

There are two basic types of park bench. One is the flat cubic mass without back, a sculptural shape, which is useful for some architectural compositions. However, it is cold, uncomfortable and should be used, if at all, in locations where people require only a moment's respite. The more comfortable bench follows the pattern of the Victorian park bench which supports the body properly, distributing weight evenly over the surface of the seat. The back of the sitter is supported well and the feet are able to rest on the ground comfortably. The bench when anthropometrically designed and properly proportioned for the human body encourages the sitter to stay, rest awhile, and admire the street or square. The location of the bench is important. It should be placed at a natural resting point on a path or in a square, but located, with its back protected, in a sheltered position from which it is possible to see interesting views and observe the activities of others while still feeling secure. It is also worth noting that steps are often used as *ad hoc* seating.

This chapter would not be complete without a note on the kiosk, a word derived from *köşk*, which in Turkish means pavilion. The Parisian kiosk used for advertisements and newstands is a most handsome method of dealing with important and useful notices which, if plastered over walls, takes on the appearance of graffiti. There are many types and uses of kiosks, the telephone box, for example, has already been mentioned. Probably the most interesting and potentially the most decorative kiosk is the bandstand. They are to be found in many European cities, often taking the form of a light circular or octagonal structure with raised platform and pyramid roof. They are usually placed in a space surrounded by benches. The form, location and surrounding space if correctly judged can create a vital, lively and decorative place in the city scene.

CONCLUSION

This chapter has dealt with the design and placement of three dimensional objects within the streets and squares of the city. The objective of the foregoing discussion was to try to understand the role of such three dimensional objects for decorating the city. Many of these objects, some being great architectural monuments, the jewels in the city's crown, are major landmarks by which we organize and

structure the city. Others are more local landmarks, special features of a locality by which we navigate and which are used to direct strangers. The furniture and fittings placed in street or square may be the great civic monument, for example, the equestrian statue, triumphal arch, monumental column or fountain. Alternatively the street furniture, like the street light or park bench, may be more utilitarian but no less important for the decoration of the city. Nevertheless, every increment of development from park bench to great fountain should be judged as an attempt to decorate the city and to establish and reinforce the identity of an area or neighbourhood as a place which is special and different.

COLOUR IN THE CITY

7

INTRODUCTION

There is a renewed interest in the use of colour, one of the most effective methods of decorating the city. Colour in the city is at the core of the subject matter of this book, the decoration of the urban realm. This chapter is the synthesis of much that has been discussed earlier. Colour should be used to strengthen the image of the city by giving emphasis to features such as landmarks, by developing colour schemes which are associated with particular districts, streets or squares and by the colour coding of street furniture.

There is great potential for polychromatic colour effects in the built environment. For much of this century the subject of colour in the city was not a matter for serious attention. A classical ideal, subscribed to by many designers, mistakenly associated with the architecture and sculpture of Ancient Greece, sees colour in architecture as a product only of natural finishes. The standing remains of ancient civilizations which have survived the ravages of time have been bleached of their original colouring by sun, wind and rain. They have, therefore, functioned as a monochromatic source of inspiration. To many the discovery that the great

monuments of antiquity were stained or painted with bright pigments has proved quite unacceptable, particularly to those with a puritanical reverence for the expression of the inherent appearance of natural materials. The facts, however, are quite clear: 'Statuary was deeply dyed with garish pigments. The marble figure of a woman found on the Athenian Acropolis was tinctured red, green, blue and yellow. Quite often statues had red lips, glowing eyes made of precious stones and even artificial eyelashes' (Porter, 1982). The Greek Temple from the point of view of colour was closer in feeling to the Chinese Temple, than to those pure but lifeless nineteenth-century copies found in many European cities.

The love of colour survives in the modern world. The church in its vestments retains a strong link with the past symbolic use of colour while colourful vivacity occasionally breaks out in the guise of the latest Parisienne or Italian fashions in women's clothes. In the environment colour was kept alive by those not schooled in the centres of artistic excellence - the working class in the suburban home, the art of the bargee, the gypsy or fairground artist. In this spirit are the monuments to Art Deco of the late 1920s and 1930s. Such buildings as those by Wallis, Gilbert and Partners for suburban London fall neatly within this populist genre. Within the

Modern Movement important experiments with colour were carried out. The De Stijl group in Holland in the early 1920s was one such group. While Mondrian used pure colours and white on canvas, containing them in a black grid of simple rectangles, Rietveld, following similar principles, decorated the internal and external planes of his architecture (Plate 7.1). Other notable modern exponents of colour in the environment include Le Corbusier who used flashes of intense primary colours to contrast with the white geometric frame of his architecture.

The legacy of the dogmatic views of Ruskin and the priggish taste in colour of those who followed abandoned the field of polychromy to the engineer. It was the engineer who embellished and protected with paint the ironwork of bridges, the coachwork of the railway engine and the working parts of industrial and agricultural machinery. Arguably it was not until the building of the Pompidou Centre by Rogers and Piano that a return was made to the more ancient architectural traditions of environmental colouring (Plate 7.2).

The natural colours of traditional settlements constructed from local material delights the eye. The sophisticated and almost pristine colouring of De Stijl gives great intellectual and emotional satisfaction. They are, however, by no means the only ways in which colour can be introduced into the environment. The case being made here is the need for a more catholic and eclectic philosophy of colour in the environment. This is particularly true now when so much of recent urban development is a 'concrete jungle'. Given the current emphasis on sustainability, many local authorities are attempting to humanize the built environment with paint, vegetation and sculpture instead of demolishing the concrete jungle.

THEORY OF COLOUR

Before discussing colour in the environment it is useful to examine the general theory of colour and to define terms used to describe and specify colours. The term colour can be used in two main ways: (i) to describe the hues of the rainbow, the constituent parts into which white light is broken (red, yellow, blue, etc.); or (ii) it can be used in its more popular form and include black, white and grey. The last three 'colours' can be obtained as paints for use in the home in the same way as red, blue or green. It is this populist definition of colour which is used in this text. It is, however, important to realize that the designer's use of colour in the environment differs from that of the painter. While following the same principles of colour harmony the urban designer is working in a field where the quality of light varies from city to city, from season to season, and from morning through to late evening. The painter, in his or her studio, attempts to mix and use colour in a constant daylight condition. The results of his or her work is exhibited in a gallery where optimum lighting conditions prevail. The painter has control over his or her palette and can chose to follow theoretical trains of thought in the abstract. The urban designer works with other actors in urban development, each following individual intentions. The urban designer works on a canvas which is three dimensional, of immense scale and in a constant process of growth and decay. The starting point for the urban designer must of necessity be the environment of the place in which he or she is working. Colour theory for the city, therefore, has to be seen in this greater context and used, where that is possible, for decorating the city by creating harmony where none may exist.

There are three sets of primary colours from which the other colours can be made. With *light* rays, red, green and blue (blue-violet) will form other hues when mixed. Red and green will form yellow: green and blue will form turquoise; red and blue will form magenta. Light primaries are additive so that all three light primaries when combined reform to produce white.

With *pigments*, red, yellow and blue are the primary colours which when combined will

Plate 7.1 Reitveld House, Utrecht, Holland

Plate 7.2 Pompidou Centre, Paris

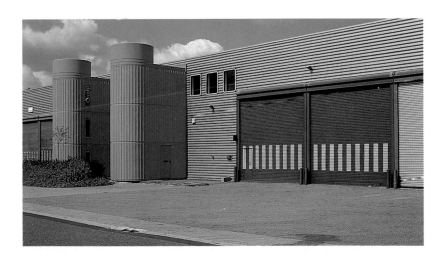

Plate 7.3 Contrasting colours at Castle Park, Nottingham

Plate 7.4 Polychromatic brickwork in a highly decorated façade, Watson Fothergill's office, Nottingham

Plate 7.5 Small area of very bright colour contrasts sharply with the main background colour in this apartment building in Hong Kong.

Plate 7.6 Campo dei Miracoli, Pisa

Plate 7 7 Grand Canal,
Venice

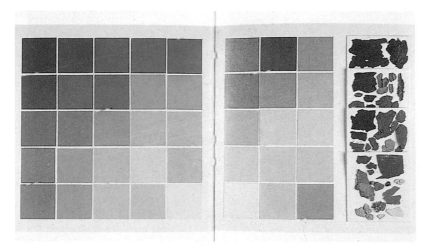

Plates 7.8 and **7.9**
Examples of the
method used by Jean-
Phillippe Lenclos in a
project in Italy. Local
materials are collected,
such as fragments of paint,
and combined with on-site
sketches in coloured pencil.
This leads to the
compilation of
representative colour
charts. From these a collage
of colour combinations are
assembled.

Plate 7.10 Cathedral, Milan

Plate 7.11 Art Nouveau façade, Prague

Plate 7.12 Art Deco façade, Bratislava

normally form other hues. Pigments tend to be subtractive, that is, red paint absorbs all light except red which is reflected from the surface. No pigments are pure mixtures, therefore, and combinations tend to deepen or subtract more of the light falling on the surface A combination of all three pigment primaries will form black or deep brown: most light falling on the surface will be absorbed and very little reflected.

In *vision*, however, there are four primaries, red, yellow, green and blue. Each of these colours, perceptually, is quite distinct from each other. Any other colours tend towards one of the primaries. That is, a mix of yellow and green would look either 'greenish' or 'yellowish'. All four colours when spun on a wheel or mixed will form grey.

The three sets of primaries of the artist, the scientist and the psychologist, each produce different colour circles. While each colour circle can be used for deciding colour harmonies, this text, for convenience, will follow the traditional circle of the artist based upon the three primary colours: red, yellow and blue.

Figure 7.1 illustrates the three-primary-colour circle of the artist. It shows the distribution of primary, secondary and tertiary colours together with the division of the colour spectrum in terms of warm and cool hues. Ives, who brought this particular spectrum to perfection suggested that the red should be magenta (*achlor*), the yellow should be clear and clean (*zanth*) and the blue should be turquoise or peacock (*cyan*). These particular primaries when mixed will give a satisfactory spectrum of pure hues (Birren, 1969).

The use of colour harmony in painting or the built environment is founded on an understanding of simultaneous and successive contrast and of the phenomena of visual colour mixtures. Chevreul (1967) described the effect of simultaneous contrast as follows: 'If we look simultaneously upon two stripes of different tones of the same colour, or upon two stripes of the same tone of different colours placed side by side . . . the eye perceives certain modifications which in the first place influence the intensity of the colour, and in the second, the optical composition of the two juxtaposed colours respectively' (Birren, 1969).

Figure 7.2 illustrates simultaneous contrast of brightness. Both greys are identical in brightness but the one seen against black appears lighter than the one seen on the white ground. Light colours will tend to heighten the depth of dark colour and dark colours will tend to make light colours lighter. Where colours of different value or brightness are placed side by side a fluted effect is produced (Figure 7.3) The edges of each tone will tend to be modified in contrary ways. The effect of 'after-image' of contrasting colours is also quite noticeable. Figure 7.4 illustrates this using black and white. The effect of contrast is best demonstrated by staring at a given hue for a short time; when the gaze is transferred to a white wall the appearance or shadow of the opposite hue is stimulated. Referring to the full colour circle (Figure 7.5) the contrasting colours are those that are diametrically opposite on the circle. The after-image of red is blue-green and vice versa; the after-image of yellow is violet and vice versa. Opposite or contrasting colours when used together tend to give brilliance and purity to each other without any change of hue. The red and green used on the Post Modern factory in Nottingham achieves this aim (Plate 7.3). The main colour for the building is mid-red which is heightened by the areas of contrasting mid-green.

Where non-complementary colours are placed side by side they are affected as if tinted by the light of the after-image of the neighbouring colour. When, for example, yellow and orange are placed together the violet after image of the yellow swings the apparent hue of the orange towards red while the blue after-image of the orange will make the yellow appear greenish.

Contrasting effects in value are stronger when light and dark colours are juxtaposed while contrasts in hue are most noticeable when the colours are close in value. However, the size of the

Figure 7.1 The red, yellow and blue colour circle
Figure 7.2 Simultaneous contrast: Each grey star is identical in brightness
Figure 7.3 Simultaneous contrast: note the 'fluted' effect where the grey tones touch each other

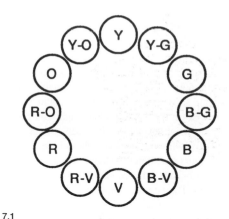

7.1

7.2

7.3

colour panels is important for contrasting effects: large panels of colour are most effective for a startling visual contrast, particularly when the contrast is both in value and hue. Strong contrasting colours in minute areas such as spots or lines become diffused by the eye and tend to conceal each other resulting in an overall dullness. Opposite colours, therefore, are most effective in contrast when used in large panels of colour. Adjacent or analogous colours on the other hand are best displayed in different minute areas. The effective use of analogous colours can be found in many traditional stone or brick walls. Each stone though from the same quarry is a slightly different hue or shade of hue. They all blend naturally together. The same effect can be found in some deeply weathered brick walls where all the bricks vary in colour but are all from analogous parts of the spectrum.

The foundation of colour harmony dates from the early nineteenth century and the work of Chevreul (1967). This theory established certain rules and principles. The first is that individual colours are beautiful in themselves; second, so are tones of the same hue; third, different hues, analogous or closely related on the colour circle, are in a harmonic relationship when they are seen in uniform or closely related tones; finally, complementary hues seen in strongly contrasting tones are also harmonious. Assorted colours when viewed through the medium of a feebly coloured glass take on a harmonic relationship.

Chevreul distinguished six distinct harmonies of colour forming two main groups: the harmonies of analogy and the harmonies of contrast. The harmonies of analogy are: (i) 'the harmony of scale' in which closely related values of a single hue are composed together; (ii) 'the harmony of hues' in which analogous colours of similar value are the basis of the composition; and (iii) 'the harmony of the dominant coloured light' in which an assortment of different hues and values are composed in a scheme as if pervaded or submerged in a dominant tinted light. The harmonies of contrast according to

Chevreul are: (iv) 'the harmony of contrast of scale' in which strongly different values of a single hue are combined; (v) 'the harmony of contrast of hues' in which related or analogous colours are exhibited in strongly different values and also in strongly different degrees of purity or chroma; and (vi) 'the harmony of contrast of colours' in which colours on opposite sides of the colour circle are combined as complements, split-complements and triad combinations.

Harmonic colour analysis for the purposes of the urban designer, for convenience, will be based upon those in Birren (1969), *Principles of Colour*. Particular attention will be paid to the harmony of modified colours. The classification that follows is a simplified version of Chevreul's work. The classification of colour harmonies to be discussed in detail will be: the harmony of adjacent colours; the harmony of opposite colours; the harmony of split-complements; the harmony of triads; the harmony of the dominant tint; and the harmony of modified colours.

THE HARMONY OF ADJACENTS

Colours tend to look good to the average viewer when they are analogous or closely related. They appear best when clearly chosen from the warm or cool side of the spectrum. Analogous colours then take on an emotional quality and contribute to mood. Analogous colours are those that sit next to each other on the colour circle. These are the colour effects that occur in nature and are found in some traditional settlements. Examples include the red to orange range of the sunset or the autumn colours varying from red to orange to yellow. Flowers exhibit the same harmonic range, the yellow nasturtium becomes deep orange at its centre and the red rose will have purple red shadows and orange red highlights. The traditional brick village in southern England has a burnt orange roof, walls with deep red stretchers and orange-red

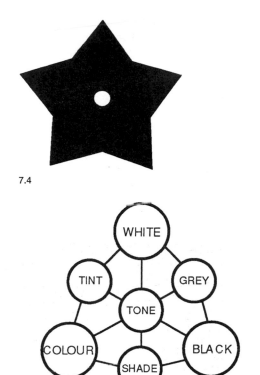

7.4

7.5

Figure 7.4 After-image: Stare at the centre of the black star for several seconds then look steadily at the black dot
Figure 7.5 Colour triangle

headers. In many Victorian areas subtly polychromatic brick and stone work combined with clay tiles produces a similarly harmonious effect.

Analogous colour effects are usually thought best when the key or central hue is a primary or secondary colour: red, blue, yellow, orange, green or violet. That is colour ranges such as red with red-violet and red-orange; orange with red-orange and yellow-orange. In these and similar instances the simple primary or secondary colour is supported and enhanced by its near neighbours. More problematic are the colour schemes where the tertiary colour is supported by its neighbours, for example yellow, yellow-orange and orange. The orange and yellow may be, perceptually, too distant and distinct to be held together by the intermediary colour, though this may be a point of personal taste. In the urban environment most colours appear in a much modified form which reduces this problem, if indeed it is a problem. Polychromatic brickwork decorated with bands or patterns in the orange to yellow range fall within this category of colour schemes (Plate 7.4). Colour arrangements of this type may look unresolved particularly when the building is aggressively new but when the brick-work weathers the colours are modified and the harshness softened.

THE HARMONY OF OPPOSITES

When complementary colours are set in strong contrast the result is found agreeable to many, exciting and vibrant to some. The harmony of opposites has a visual quality which is intellectual. The harmony of opposites usually juxtaposes a warm colour against a cool one, that is, enhancing the positive quality of the warm colour with the passive quality of the cool one. Complementary colours are found diametrically opposite each other on the colour circle, for example, blue and orange, or green and red. Due to the law of simultaneous contrast, each of the pairs of complementary colours heighten the intensity of the other. In nature this is a colour scheme often found in birds, butterflies and flowers, examples are the violet flower with yellow centre or the blue bird with orange flash. In the Algarve, an orange sunset is often seen against a deep blue sky. In the built environment one must turn to a less sophisticated setting to find this exciting colour combination. Some of the cottages of the Mediterranean countries have red shuttered windows juxtaposed against a green frame and set within whitewashed walls. The use of blue and gold on medieval vault-ing in Cathedrals such as Canterbury uses this

heightened intensity of the colours to impress the viewers even from the lofty height of the nave ceiling.

The harmony of opposites includes also black set against white. Such an achromatic scheme is of great sophistication, a cerebral rather than emotional response to colour. For natural examples of this colour harmony, one must turn to the northern European countries when the landscape is covered with snow, the sky drained of colour and the shapes of trees stand out in stark black contrast. In northern Europe, particularly in Britain, there is a long tradition of black and white buildings, Chester being a particularly fine example.

THE HARMONY OF SPLIT-COMPLEMENTS

In the harmony of split-complements a key colour is combined with the two hues that lie next to its exact opposite on the colour circle. Examples would include red with yellow-green and blue-green; red-orange with green and blue; and orange with blue-green and blue-violet. As with adjacents the primaries and secondaries (red, yellow, blue, orange, green and violet) probably look better with split-complements than do the tertiary colours. This, however, may be a matter of personal preference. The result is more sophisticated and less direct than the simple harmony of complements. It offers the opportunity to attain greater variety and subtlety into the colour scheme, an important requirement in decorating the city.

THE HARMONY OF TRIADS

This harmony offers the possibility of a wider palette for the designer and one that may be partic-ularly useful for the urban designer in particular. The basis of the triad is a choice of three equally spaced colours in the spectrum which produce a weighty balance. There are four triad possibilities:

the primaries, red, yellow, blue; the secondaries, orange, green, violet, the intermediaries (tertiaries), red-orange, yellow-green, and blue-violet; and another group of tertiaries, yellow-orange, blue-green and red-violet. The primary triad of red, yellow, blue is primitive, direct and normally has a universal unsophisticated charm. Used however with white, as Le Corbusier did, it then takes on a highly sophisticated quality. The combinations of intermediary or tertiary hues is violent and startling. Chinese temples exhibit colour schemes of this type based upon a widely spaced triad of colours (Plate 7.5).

THE HARMONY OF THE DOMINANT TINT

The colours of nature and those fashioned by man, are commonly seen under conditions of tinted light. Distant landscapes may be enveloped in a greyish or purplish mist or a distant hilltown tinted by the pink of early dawn. The city, too, may be marked by the haze of heat or less pleasurably by the pall of pollution. Hong Kong Island seen from Kowloon at times rises from a pale cream light softening the colours of the structures whether they be the traditional stone of early colonial buildings or the structural frames of the Hong Kong and Shanghai Bank. Artists have been aware of these effects and have experimented with harmony produced by the influence of an all-pervading hued tint. A normal series of colours when washed over with a transparent tint will harmonize colours of wide disparity. A yellow tint will shift the original ground colours towards a warm sunny harmony; a blue tint moves the ground colour towards a moonlight effect. The method almost guarantees a concordant and harmonious result regardless of how crude the underneath colours may be before they are tinted. This is a most fortunate phenomenon for the urban designer. Nevertheless it is important to know the precise tinting effects of the micro-climate at various times and seasons so that those tints can be reinforced using a concordant background of colour and

materials. The pale milky white of Paris, for example, is in part due to its atmosphere but it is strengthened and enhanced by the pale grey of its architecture and the black trim of its ironwork.

THE HARMONY OF MODIFIED COLOURS

The colour triangle along with the colour circle are the two most important tools of the artist for colour analysis and the harmonic control of the palette. The colour triangle consists of a pure hue, taken from the colour circle, and placed at one point of the triangle, white is placed at the second point and black at the third point of the triangle. Within this triangle it is possible to arrange sequentially all the *tints*, *tones* and *shades* of the chosen hue. A triangle can be constructed for all pure hues. Along the side of the triangle from the hue, say clear red, to white are arranged the *tints* of red, becoming paler until white is reached. Along the second side are the *shades* of red getting darker until they reach black. Along the third side of the triangle are the *greys*, that is, a transition from black to white. From the various greys back to red would be the *tones* of red. A *tint*, therefore, is a mixture of pure colour and white. A *shade* is a mixture of pure colour and black. A *tone* is a mixture of pure colour, black and white. *Grey* is a mixture of black and white.

In combining colours for a design whether it is a painting or an environmental colour scheme it is usually thought that hues light in value as pure colours, make the best tints. Hues that are normally dark in value as pure colours make the best shades. If this is true then tints would be confined to yellow, orange, yellow-orange, green and yellow-green, while the shades used would be from red, red-violet, violet, blue-violet and blue. This, however, may be another case of personal taste for many would admire the pale pinks and pastel blues of the country cottages of some coastal villages, while others would prefer the use of white in such places. The basis for this rule is one of natural harmony so that pale yellow, pale orange, deep red and deep violet would be thought to look well together. The reverse would look unnatural and discordant. Yellow as a shade becomes deep olive, orange becomes brown, red becomes a strong pink and violet becomes lavender. While the first range may not be to everyone's taste the second would appear discordant to most.

For the urban designer it is the harmony achieved with modified hues together with the harmony of the dominant tint which is of particular importance. The environment in general and the city in particular is made up of modified colours masked by atmospheric tints associated with the time of day and the particular season. The colours found in the city rarely approximate to pure colour and when such colours appear they are normally small highlights, the bright red pillar box, the Algarvian blue trim around the doors and windows of the traditional home, or the brightly painted doors of the sombre Victorian terrace. The natural building materials, such as stone, brick and earth tend to be modified and subtle hues. It is to the environment that the urban designer often turns for ideas, and the natural environment in general consists mainly of the more subtle colours.

The world of colour as a scientific phenomenon consists of a limitless and infinite number of different colours. Judged in terms such as wavelength, luminance and degrees of reflectance there are literally millions of colours. There is a great difference between this scientific world of colour and the experiential world of human sensation. Colours distinguished by the eye are limited to less than a few thousand. In terms of the pure light of the spectrum the eye cannot distinguish more than 180 different hues. Using dyes or pigments still fewer would be distinguished. However, when spectral colours are modified with white, black or grey a whole new series of colours become distinguishable as, for example, pinks, browns and navys.

The eye does not respond to stimulation like a scientific instrument; it is a mental response which allocates colours to categories. The eye does not see an infinite number of colours in the spectrum, the colours are categorized into red, yellow, blue, green and colours that bear resemblance to them. Similarly colours grading from a pure hue, say red, to white are simplified from an infinite number of steps to a group of colours which are red then a sudden jump to a group that are pink and a final jump to white. Similarly orange may be scaled down towards black with a sudden jump to the browns then to black.

The eye constantly struggles to bring order to colour classification from a world which is chaotic. The reaction to colour to a great extent, therefore, is personal and also to some extent culturally determined. We group colours in ways which have been given to us during the process of socialization. This is not simply the way in which colours are categorized but also the whole process of giving meaning to colour. The constant theme in this personalized classification of colour is the need to simplify the world of colour. If indeed complexity and fine colour discrimination were the objective then the dictionaries would be filled with words describing colour. In fact in English there are only a few primitive and specialized words for colours: red, yellow, green, blue, black and white. Most other words for colours are borrowed: violet, orchid, lilac, rose are from flowers; emerald, ruby, turquoise from stones, while cherry, lemon, lime, chocolate, olive, peach are all from foods.

In this infinitely complex world of colour it is the task of the designer to take this need for simplicity and to further order and structure colour so that it is comprehensible to the average viewer. The great artist usually limits his or her palette to a few of those colours distinguishable by human sight. This limited palette is the foundation of composition; simplicity is a necessity for appreciation. In theory any of the tones, shades or tints of a hue can be used in a composition – they are all harmonic. The primary colour can also be used with black, white or grey. It is often thought desirable to further restrict the palette within the triangle shown in Figure 7.5 to one of the following series: black, grey and white; pure colour, tint and white; pure colour, shade and black; tint, tone and shade; tint, tone and black; tint, tone and shade; tint, or shade, tone and white. The older parts of cities such as Venice or Pisa, popular with tourists, are composed of buildings constructed mainly from materials found in the region. The range of colours of these materials are usually from a band within the much wider spectrum of the rainbow. Furthermore the colours of materials used in such traditional cities are usually modified hues, tones, tints and shades. Pure colour, when used, emphasizes and highlights special features and is confined to small areas. Contrast is provided by nature with a bright blue sky or a dark green lawn (Plates 7.6 and 7.7).

THE USE OF COLOUR IN THE CITY

Until the nineteenth century, European cities developed slowly employing indigenous materials from their regions for the building envelope. Architectural styles changed but the building materials did not. The constant use of local materials produced street, squares and whole cities with great visual harmony despite the varied forms. In this way the colour of the city was established and is an aspect of its history which has not been completely submerged by nineteenth- and twentieth-century developments. In Oxford's High Street many styles are reflected but all have been unified by scale, material and especially colour. The colour of Oxford is derived from the ochres of the yellow sandstone. In the traditional city there was easy access to cheap earth pigments for painting stucco façades. Even in the nineteenth century it was only the wealthy who could afford the brighter 'imported' or 'foreign' colours for doors and windows. Cities and regions have come to be associated with particular colour ranges: 'For instance, the ochres and reds of Lyons; and, among

the blues and reds, the predominance of a "Maria Theresa" yellow in central Vienna. . . . There are also the brickdust reds and Georgian greens of a revamped Savannah, the pinks of Suffolk and Devon cottages, and the brilliant reds, blues and yellows of houses on the Adriatic island of Burano' (Porter, 1982). The problem posed for the urban designer is how to recapture such colour schemes and give individuality and distinction back to each centre.

Turin in 1800 set up a Council of Builders to devise and implement a colour plan for the city. The idea was to colour principal streets and squares characterized by a unified architecture in a co-ordinated scheme. The Council devised a series of chromatic pathways for the major processional routes to Turin's centre, Piazza Castello. The colour scheme for each route was based upon popular city colours and was implemented through permissions given for redecoration applications. It is not known how long the original colour scheme lasted but it was praised by Nietzsche in the late nineteenth century and by Henry James in the early twentieth century.

In his work on colour in the environment Jean-Philippe Lenclos (1977) has developed the ideas found in Turin's earlier experiment (Düttmann, et al., 1981). He has aimed to preserve a sense of place by devising a palette of colours relating to particular localities in France. Lenclos collects colour samples from sites within the region - fragments of paint, materials from walls, doors, shutters, together with natural elements such as moss, lichen, rock and earth. He analyses and structures the colours he finds to form a colour map for the region and a palette for intervention in the built environment (Porter, 1982) (Plates 7.8 and 7.9).

The lessons that can be learnt from Turin and Lenclos are twofold. First an environmental survey is necessary to establish a colour map of the region or city and from that colour map palettes established as the basis for colour schemes. Second, any colour scheme for a city should be comprehensive and capable of implementation. From earlier sections of the chapter it would seem desirable that any colour scheme established should follow the laws of harmonic colour composition.

There are four different scales on which colour in the city can be seen: (i) the scale of the city or of the district; (ii) the scale of the street or square, where colour can create various characteristics or moods depending on adjacent buildings, and at street corners or on diametrically opposed façades; (iii) the scale of the individual buildings; and (iv) the scale of details - windows, shutters, ironwork, street furnishings. Furthermore colour in streets and on buildings can be seen in four different ways: (i) from the side; (ii) from the front; (iii) from above; and (iv) from below. It can be seen in deep shadow, in conditions of blazing sunshine or harshly against a bright sky. In each condition the same pigment may take on a different shade, tint or tone of the same hue.

Milan is a city which has a clearly defined colour pattern. It is a highly sophisticated and unique use of colour. Cities like Siena, Florence and Bologna depend for their colour on materials such as brick, terracotta and marble. In Florence, for example, dark colours abound including the dark green marble cladding of the Cathedral. It is a city of shades and tones. In Siena the light and rather beautifully decorated Cathedral decorates a totally different space from the dark coloured main square and the dark cliff-like streets that connect the Cathedral and the main square. Dark brick and terracotta are the colours of the arcaded streets and squares in Bologna where rich gold is splashed on the soffit and arch of vaulted arcades. However, in Milan the experience of colour is quite different: here dark and light colours are juxtaposed. It is a city of light and shade. The highly decorated Cathedral provides a white focus to the main square which has dark colours to the south and light pinks to the north. This highlighting of different areas in the city with white marble clad buildings is a theme repeated throughout the city. The deeply shadowed cloisters of St Amblogio are contrasted with the brightness of the white marble clad Mausoleum. In Piazza Fontana white figurines are used to highlight the terracotta decorations while in Piazza della Scala white is used in such a way that the space appears to expand. The use of pink and elaborate decorations surrounding doors and windows is a common feature of main roads leading to the south and west of the Piazza Duomo. Pink and grey is used with great care and delicacy, areas of colour being framed with marble or travertine. The pink in streets leading to the Duomo echoes the theme of an important enclosing wall in the square and is a subtle preparation for the Cathedral surrounds. On Via Carducci, white is used on the Palazzo Nuovo to emphasize the corner with a highly decorative loggia. In Milan colour is used both to decorate and to highlight. The use of white to exploit the position of important city nodes and landmarks is a particularly clever use of colour in the city, in addition to being highly decorative (Plate 7.10).

In Vienna and Prague, yellow is the colour used to highlight Baroque landmarks. Small Baroque churches usually along narrow streets become visually significant when painted yellow. Colour of such intensity when combined with movements of surface shadows becomes highly decorative without being elaborate. In both Prague and Bratislava elaborately coloured decorations are common in Art Nouveau and Art Deco façades (Plates 7.11 and 7.12). Colour on buildings from both periods is widely used over façades, and while intricate and pleasing to the casual observer, it nevertheless misses the opportunity for the strategic use of colour and decoration which earlier and more disciplined periods achieved. For instance, in Buda the Cathedral is a good example of colour used to highlight a landmark and important symbol of community solidarity. The Cathedral stands out in marked contrast to the dark shades and tones of red, green and yellow used along the nearby medieval streets.

The two most common urban spaces are the street and square. The colour scheme of the street or square may have a considerable effect upon its character and appearance. It can contribute to the unity of the street or square, or it may destroy that unity. In addition, the colours used in the street have in themselves the ability to create character and mood. Taking the street for example, it is possible to emphasize the wall planes of the street by painting them a light tone (Figure 7.6). Alternatively the volume of the street can be emphasized by colouring the façades the same tone as the dark pavement, or the length of the street could be emphasized by horizontal strips along the façades (Figure 7.7). The street can also be broken down into units with vertical bands of colouring (Figure 7.8). Whichever scheme is followed the street should be viewed strategically as an element in the city, a path leading from node to node and interspersed with landmark features and street corners. It is features such as these which should influence the final distribution of colour within the street.

Figure 7.7 Colour scheme emphasizing a street's volume

Figure 7.6 Colour emphasizing a street's wall planes

Figure 7.8 Colour scheme emphasizing the verticality of a street's façades

When developing a colour scheme for a building it must first be seen in its strategic relationship with its immediate surroundings. The building's visual function within the city or district should also be established. For example is the building an important landmark or a closure to a vista? Does the building lie upon an important path with a particular colour coding? Having decided the strategic requirements then the building itself can be examined: if it is rich in decoration it will be articulated with relief – cornices, window-frames, niches, projecting bays and oriels, stairwells, corner mouldings, overhanging roofs, balconies, etc. The relief lies in front of the main wall surface and is foreground colour, the wall becomes the ground or background colour. The background may be dark with pale relief or vice versa, but some distinction is necessary for articulation.

When choosing a colour scheme for a building it is the details that are the final constructional elements to receive consideration. It is only when we stop and concentrate the gaze do we notice the details and colours of fixtures and fittings but they are important for the overall effect of the street and where possible if flanking an important route they should be co-ordinated. The three zones of the building, the base, the middle zone and the roof zone, together with the relief and detailing make up the architectural treatment of the street. The planes,

projections and ornamental work can be emphasized to create a lively pattern of decoration. In other areas where for strategic or masterplan reasons the street can be bland and unassuming then the difference in elements can be masked by the subtle use of shades, tones or tints of the same colour.

CONCLUSION

Colour is one of the most important aspects of city life: it is one of the main factors in our description of a city's decorative effect. To be fully effective for city decoration requires some strategic policy which sets a colour agenda for the city and its main elements, districts, paths nodes, edges and landmarks (Lynch, 1960). The city image from the point of view of colour is often formed over a long history and also strongly affected by its environmental setting. Determination of colour image requires a sensitive response from the urban designer. A response which should be based on a thorough survey of colour in the local environment. For the remainder of the city, colour can be used to highlight important buildings and landmarks, colour code important paths and give individuality within the overall pattern for important squares and meeting places.

CONCLUSION
THE CITY OF TODAY AND TOMORROW: ORNAMENT AND DECORATION

8

INTRODUCTION

The theme of this book is the role, form and location of ornament and decoration in the city. The thesis presented is the notion that each increment of development should be seen as an attempt to decorate the city. It is through the successful use of decoration that, in Alexander's terms, the city can be 'healed' or 'made whole' (Alexander, 1987). Decoration can unify the disparate elements in the urban realm. It has been argued that successful decoration results from an understanding of its function, where function is used in its broadest sense to include symbol and sign. Decoration is not, however, an aesthetic activity divorced from the realities and practicalities of everyday life in the city. The city is a place of residence, work, commerce, industry, leisure and education. As such it has its own developmental imperatives. The urban designer would be unwise to disregard these forces at work in the city. The urban designer may be able to mould and shape these forces beneficially but never completely control them.

THE MODERN CITY

Modernist architecture, in its puritanical zeal, rejected ornament and decoration: arguably it denied the city the possibility of a richer and enriching environment. The rational modernist mind which neatly compartmentalized activities of the urban environment into discrete zones rejected both the complexity of urban life and the rich traditions of urban design. The city was considered a machine to provide work, housing and other activities connected by roads not streets. Le Corbusier, by rejecting the street and square, was clearly rejecting a great European tradition of city building (Le Corbusier, 1946; 1947). Le Corbusier was an artist, a great architect, who could never understand and come to terms with the city in all its complexity. Those who followed his ideas of raising concrete boxes on pilotis, continued the tradition of rejecting urban spaces, while failing to replicate the sculptural elegance that many of his buildings achieved. Unlike Renaissance or Baroque masters few of the Modern masters understood or

8.1

8.2

Figure 8.1 Town Hall,
Saynatsalo
Figure 8.2 Flats, Lenton,
Nottingham

cared for urban design: their commitment was to the individual building. Even the humanist among the Modern masters, Alvar Aalto rarely managed to create rewarding urban spaces. The Town Hall in Saynatsalo is a delightful exception where an intimate urban space is created with simple modern elements decorated by fine brickwork (Figure 8.1).

Many of the architects associated with the Modern Movement expressed their interpretation of socialism more in designs for cities than in their architecture. This understanding of socialism led to a puritanical zeal which defined the basic needs of the masses as adequate housing, work, etc. In addition, the masses would be protected from the decadence of the late nineteenth century urban environment that epitomized the taste and dominance of the bourgeoisie. Furthermore, it was argued that the construction of pre-fabricated

buildings with the streamlined elegance of the machine would bring great architecture to all. The individually designed, crafted and embellished building was to be a thing of the past. Unfortunately the result was not the brave new world of the utopian architect. The masses were allocated a shoe box in the sky, which was all the state could provide (Figure 8.2). The brave new world was closer to the chiding of Betjemin:

Remove those cottages, a huddled throng!
Too many babies have been born in there,
Too many coffins, bumping down the stair . . .

I have a Vision of the Future, chum,
The workers' flats in fields of soya beans
Tower up like silver pencils, score on score.
And surging Millions hear the challenge come
From microphones in communal canteens
'No right! No wrong! All's perfect evermore'.

In Britain the full development of Modern Architecture never quite materialized, or rather was fully realized only by a small number of practices on a few occasions. Many of the ideas and ideals of the 'Modern Movement' were compromised and diluted in the conservative social climate of this country. Planners in Britain followed quite a different educational path from their architectural colleagues. The values planners held were influenced by Geddes, Howard, Abercrombie and Mumford and their aesthetic sensibilities formed by the ideas of Sitte and Unwin (Geddes, 1949; Howard, 1965; Abercrombie, 1944; Mumford, 1938; Sitte, 1901; Unwin, 1909). As a group, the planning profession were part of the establishment and tended to follow a 'middle of the road' political stance. The architect/planners, those responsible for the New Towns and major public developments in the 1950s and 1960s, sat rather uneasily between the two philosophies. Zoning, the need for roads and an efficient transport network, a multi-storey solution to density problems and modern structures were largely accepted by the New Town designers and the city architects in charge of redevelopment. A number of architect/planners, such as Gibberd and Holford, accepted the writings of Sitte and tried the impossible task of integrating them with the more revolutionary architectural ideas originating in Europe. In many instances the results were not successful. In Britain these ideas helped to shape the new towns and large scale redevelopment required after the war. Two such examples are the rebuilt town centre at Coventry by Gibson and the completely New Town centre in Harlow by Gibberd (Figure 8.3). Both schemes attempted to build urban spaces based on the ideas of Sitte. They failed for a number of reasons: the urban spaces formed in the development were surrounded by a single use or by uses which died at night; the precincts were isolated from the rest of the urban area by heavily trafficked roads and car parks; the architecture was faceless and without distinction; the idea of the multi-function, crowded and busy street was rejected. The

8.3

8.4

Figure 8.3 Town centre, Stevenage
Figure 8.4 Paternoster Square, London

Figure 8.5 Street scene, Mykonos
Figure 8.6 Street scene, Germany

8.5

8.6

result was a series of largely unoccupied, cold and wind swept public areas. Another example of post-war Modernist urban design that Postmodernists criticize is the Paternoster Square development in London by Holford. The spaces originally planned as an informal Sittesque landscape around St Paul's Cathedral suffer from the same defects as the town centre at Harlow. In this case, the result was compounded by the Church Commissioners who wanted to maximize floor space and therefore profit (Figure 8.4).

These stark environments were not only without decoration and ornament but also failed to achieve the simple elegance of spaces found in Greece, Italy and other parts of the Mediterranean. In the traditional towns of Southern Europe small scale spaces are enlivened with a few well placed hanging baskets, doors and windows that decorate street and square, signs, fountains and sculpture that enrich the urban scene (Figure 8.5). Northern Europe too is not without its tradition of delightfully decorative public squares and streets (Figure 8.6).

The loss of this great tradition cannot, however, be laid entirely at the feet of Modernist architects and planners. This would be to invest the respective professions with too much power. Other more powerful forces were at work denuding the city of its traditional character (Figure 8.7). Post-modern urbanists must understand the social, political and economic forces which are at work in the city if they are to propose the creation of a more decorated city. There can be no going back to some ideal time in the past except for inspiration. Mere copying would be pastiche (Figure 8.8). It is also to the future city and its role and function that the urbanist must look for the rational basis of a decorative public realm of human scale, even if the forms and concepts used for the decoration derive from past traditions.

An exhaustive analysis of the forces acting upon the city and conditioning its development. has been presented elsewhere for example, (Mumford, 1938; 1944; 1946; 1961; Ravetz, 1980 and Ambrose,

1979). It would not be appropriate in a book on ornament and decoration to repeat that analysis. However, it is necessary to outline, briefly, those factors which may have a bearing upon the creation of a decorated city.

In North America and western Europe the twin values of democracy and the free market predominate. The ensuing importance given to individualism, competition and the profit motive has an inexorable effect upon city form. Planners, architects and urban designers can work with these main currents, controlling and possibly mitigating some of their worst effects or stand like an impotent Canute bidding the tide to retreat.

One result of western cultural patterns is cities where the land market conditions the height of buildings and the location of activities. Where land values are high, usually at important centres or communication nodes, densities are high. Single uses tend to dominate in these areas because of economies of scale and the locational advantage of proximity to allied or associated business. In contrast the periphery of many cities is expanding outwards with low density suburbs. For example, in Britain and other property owning democracies the ideal of owning a house with a garden dominates the ambition of most families. This demand is met by the development of low density single use housing suburbs. Industrial, business, shopping and leisure parks follow the population to suburban locations. In Britain the trend is facilitated by road dominated transport policies supported by a largely compliant electorate.

The building industry is an important part of the commercial democracy and follows the same imperatives. Buildings are constructed for profit. Traditional materials such as stone, brick and slate are expensive. The craftsmanship to mould such materials into decorative patterns is also expensive as is on site construction. Buildings, if they are to be reduced in cost and therefore maximize profits, tend to be constructed of standard prefabricated, factory-made components requiring little fixing on

8.7

8.8

Figure 8.7 Market Square, Nottingham
Figure 8.8 Richmond Riverside, London

the site. Where decoration or expensive materials are used it is to express commercial strength; it symbolizes the power and prestige of the enterprise, usually a multi-national organization. Buildings, their materials and components, have been internationalized with a corresponding loss of the rich regional identity associated with the traditional city. Modern architects and planners tried to harness these technological forces for the benefit of the general population. In doing so they formulated a 'machine aesthetic' for the building and the city. When seen in this light, the failure of the modern city, is a failure of a society and its culture, of which the design and planning professions are only a small part.

Amongst the well documented failings of the modern city are, for example, the growing congestion on the roads including the danger of gridlock; the dangerous conditions of city life; isolation in the suburbs, an underclass of poor and disenfranchised people; a dying city centre; and an ageing city infrastructure. The inner city has become an area of social and economic deprivation with a shrinking tax base from which to solve its problems. These local difficulties have to be seen against the more serious world problems of pollution, ozone layer depletion, the greenhouse effect and climate change, resource depletion, levels of energy consumption, population growth, worldwide food shortages and famine (Myers, 1987). Paradoxically, these seemingly insurmountable world problems may stimulate a change in the ethos of society and its values. Such change in attitudes may be necessary to save the city and bring about a return to its prime function as the home of humankind, a place that does not possess the image of a fearsome object from which all sane people flee.

A SUSTAINABLE FUTURE

There is a growing international consensus that all development in the future should be sustainable.

Sustainable development has many definitions. A common definition is: 'to meet the needs of the current generation without preventing future generations meeting their needs' (Brundtland, 1987). The adoption of sustainability as the guiding principle for development policy formulation has a number of implications for the city and its form.

The definition of sustainable development used here implies both inter- and intra-generational equity. Leaving aside for a moment, equity between nations, the definition does require a radical rethink of the distribution of wealth within a given society. Job creation in the service, leisure and quality-of-life industries may be a part of this process of equitable resource distribution. If that proves to be true then the decorative work for the city by artists, craftsman or production on the factory floor may once again be on the urban design agenda.

Sustainability implies the careful husbandry of the natural and man-made environment. It implies a return to the mores of farming traditions, that is, leaving the land in a better condition than it was found. This value of good husbandry applies to the built as well as the natural environment. Conservation of building stock becomes, under this regime, the norm, while demolition and reconstruction is the strategy requiring justification. There seems a broad consensus for the conservation of the rich urban heritage in many European cities. Because of conservation policies much that is currently of architectural and historical value in our cities will probably be retained. Conservation of the built environment, more generally, however, may become more commonplace. Not simply for reasons of history, aesthetics or sentiment, but in order to reduce energy consumption, waste and resource depletion. In that scenario many buildings currently considered unsuitable, unsightly or downright ugly would be found new uses and humanized with a decorative treatment of the façade and the surrounding environment.

For reasons of energy efficiency, additions to the sustainable city of the future may take the form of low-rise, high density developments sited along corridors of infrastructure and public transport (Owens, 1991). Super-insulated three and four storey mixed use buildings, constructed from regional materials would provide urban designers with a new agenda for design (Blowers, 1993). The rich texture of urban space resulting from such urban policies opens up a wide field for decoration with planting, floorscape and street furniture. The use of 'long-life' traditional facing materials for buildings also offers scope for a decorative architecture.

A greater reliance on public transport as opposed to the universal use of the private motor car is necessary for energy conservation, particularly for the reduction of the use of fossil fuels (Matthew and Rodwell, 1991). A viable public transport system is also necessary if the city is to avoid congestion on a scale requiring massive urban surgery and investment to solve the problems of mass movement. A number of cities in Europe, meanwhile, are investing in public transport, restraining the use of the car and emphasizing movement by foot, bicycle, bus, tram or train. Assuming this trend will continue, then life for the city centre and other important nodes looks bright. The revitalization of the centre offers the urban designer the greatest scope for the use of decorative talents. It is here that the community has traditionally concentrated most of its creative energy. Change to a more sustainable society and the development of urban structures worthy of the values inherent in such a society requires a major paradigm shift in the way we think about cities. While there are signs of this cultural change (necessary, some would say, for human survival) these signs are by no means universal or clearly evident. Catastrophe may be necessary to propel society in the direction of this paradigm shift and its concomitant technological changes.

THE POST-MODERN CITY

Before outlining a strategy for future city decoration it is appropriate to examine some examples of the

Figure 8.9 The Portland Building, Portland, Oregon

1980s urban spaces which have done so much to re-establish the pleasure of walking along streets and sitting in the calm of a city square. Portland, Oregon, as a city, made a concerted effort to bring people back to its centre. In Portland the flagship of this process was the celebrated town hall which, through the use of various Post-modern idioms, created a decorated landmark. The building contains many fine sculptures, a feature which is repeated in the surrounding streets. The animal sculptures which dominate the main street and the square continue to please the residents long after their novelty has worn off. Another means of bringing vitality back to the downtown area was the creation of a public square by the demolition of a city block. The square cleverly uses the slope of the land to

8.10

8.11

Figure 8.10 Pioneer Courthouse Square, Portland, Oregon

Figure 8.11 Street decorated with animal sculptures, Portland, Oregon

create a multi-functional space surrounded by sculptures which both define and enclose it. The quality of the environment is further enhanced by the use of water which helps to create a pleasant microclimate in the heart of a busy city. There is a total design effort in this part of Portland, its aim being to heal the city (Figures 8.9 to 8.11).

The 16th Street Mall in Denver, Colorado, also illustrates the use of a decorated environment to enrich and bring life back to a dying downtown. Having lost its heart it was decided to create an urban shopping mall in the downtown area. The new downtown shopping mall had to compete with suburban malls which have a distinct locational advantage for the motorist. To compete successfully the developers employed a range of urban design skills in the production of an attractive shopping street. Sixteenth Street is an example of total environmental design where the most notable and unifying element of decoration is the floorscape which is complemented by well-designed utilitarian street furniture. A clever dimension of this total design is the use of simple unadorned glass façades which decorate the street through changing reflections of floorscape, colourful window displays and their illumination of the street after dark. A safe, controlled environment has been created. The small shopping arcades provide a natural surveillance for the street beyond the glazing while richly decorating the environment with a constantly changing display of both goods and shoppers (Figures 8.12 and 8.13).

The Zeil in Frankfurt is a similar development to the 16th Street Mall in Denver. Like Denver, it is a pedestrian shopping mall where there has been an attempt to 'heal' or 'make whole' the city centre through the use of floorscape, utilitarian street furniture, sculpture and trees. Yet this development is not as successful as that in Denver. The Zeil is too wide and the floor paving fails to unify the scheme successfully. The inhuman scale and barren lack of unity in the 1950s and 1960s buildings which front onto the Zeil deny it the qualities of the 16th Street Mall in Denver (Figure 8.14).

8.12

8.13

Figure 8.12 Sixteenth Street Mall, Denver
Figure 8.13 Sixteenth Street Mall, Denver

8.14

8.15

Broadgate in the City of London is an example of fine urban development accomplished by using a mixture of Modern and Post-modern design elements. The area is decorated by building façades which enclose a variety of squares. The public spaces are also used for the location of sculpture giving human scale to them. Broadgate contains two contrasting styles of city decoration. It has a 'high-tech' but decorative environment and also a deriva-tive Post-modern decorative environment. Deciding which part of the development is most successful is a matter for individual taste. The effort to decorate the urban realm in both cases is a commendable achievement (Figures 8.15 to 8.17). The decorative quality of the spaces is in stark contrast to the grey foreboding of Paternoster Square near St Paul's Cathedral.

In Birmingham there has been another major effort to revive a city centre and regain civic pride. Having been devastated by the intervention of the traffic engineer, Modernist architecture and the voracious commercial interests which spawned the humiliation of the 'Bull Ring', the city authorities are trying to counteract a past planning failure. Once again the main element used in this effort to revive the centre is a combination of an attractive floorscape, carefully selected street furniture and civic sculpture. The redesigned square uses sculpture, water and a changing ground plane to create a richly decorated multi-functional civic area.

Birmingham plans to create other new squares endowed with sculpture and enclosed by decorated façades. The austerity of the Modernist city is being rejected. Where possible the city is being remodelled in order to create a humane and decorated environment which has the approval of the general public (Figures 8.18 and 8.19).

CONCLUSION

Ornament and decoration in the city is expensive and involves the use of scarce human and material resources; it must, therefore, be used with economy and discretion. As a consequence some places in the city will be more decorative than others; some locations will be less decorated. The location of decoration should be part of a plan so that its impact can be maximized. A strategy and policy for the colour and decorative scheme for a city is a prime requirement for healing or unifying the city. Such a strategy could be based upon a Lynch type study; decoration being used to emphasize districts, paths, nodes, edges and landmarks (Lynch, 1960). Each city district should be analysed to reveal the colours and decorative effects which distinguish it from neighbouring areas and the details discovered therein, used as a basis for any future developments. The city paths and nodes should each be analysed to discover those elements of façade, floorscape and furniture by which they are currently distinguished. These local visual themes should be reinforced by all new additions. The city's landmarks and edges are locations where ornament can be used to great effect. It is on these special features that urban designers of the past have often used a wealth of decoration, for example, the great sculptural roofs associated with landmarks or the dramatic quayside landscaping of the waterfront.

Ornament and decoration whether it is on façade or floor plane, whether it is in street or square is of limited expanse compared with the undecorated backcloth. Its location has to be chosen with care.

8.16

8.17

Figure 8.16 Leaping Hare, Broadgate, London
Figure 8.17 Broadgate, London

155

Figure 8.18 Centenary
Square, Birmingham
Figure 8.19 Victoria
Square, Birmingham

8.18

A number of possible locations have been outlined
in previous chapters. Ornament and decoration is
most effective when its use is governed by some
rationale. The rationale for decoration is often of a
functional nature, for example, at the junction of
material change, to outline the edge of a building
element such as a window or to emphasize change
of plane or ownership. Once a decorative theme is
established it gives reason for the distribution of
decoration for additions to the urban scene. There
has been no attempt here to educate the taste of
the reader nor to dictate a style of decoration. Such
matters are questions only for the individual. It has
been the aim of this book to put forward principles
for the rational location and distribution of
ornament and decoration; principles, however,
which are flexible enough to permit creative interpretation.

8.19

BIBLIOGRAPHY

Abercrombie, P. (1914) 'The Era of Architectural Town Planning', *Town Planning Review*, Vol. 5 (1) pp. 195-213.

Abercrombie, P. (1933, reprinted 1944) *Town and Country Planning*, London: Butterworth.

Adshead, S.D. (1911a) 'The Decoration and Furnishing of the City: Introduction', *Town Planning Review*. Vol. 2 (1) pp. 16-21.

Adshead, S.D. (1911b) 'The Decoration and Furnishing of the City: No. 2. Monumental Columns', *Town Planning Review*, Vol. 2 (2) pp. 95-98.

Adshead, S.D. (1911c) 'The Decoration and Furnishing of the City: No 3. Obelisks', *Town Planning Review*, Vol. 2 (3) pp. 197-199.

Adshead, S.D. (1912a) 'The Decoration and Furnishing of the City: No. 4. Clock Monuments', *Town Planning Review*, Vol. 2 (4) pp. 302-304.

Adshead, S.D. (1912b) 'The Decoration and Furnishing of the City: No. 5. Fountains', *Town Planning Review*, Vol. 3 (1) pp. 19-22.

Adshead, S.D. (1912c) 'The Decoration and Furnishing of the City: No. 6. Fountains', *Town Planning Review*, Vol. 3 (2) pp. 114-117.

Adshead, S.D. (1912d) 'The Decoration and Furnishing of the City: No. 7. Statuary', *Town Planning Review*, Vol. 3 (3) pp. 171-175.

Adshead, S.D. (1913a) 'The Decoration and Furnishing of the City: No. 8. Statuary The Single Figure and the Group', *Town Planning Review*, Vol. 3 (4) pp. 238-243.

Adshead, S.D. (1913b) 'The Decoration and Furnishing of the City: No. 9. Equestrian Statues', *Town Planning Review*, Vol. 4 (1) pp. 3-6.

Adshead, S.D. (1913c) 'The Decoration and Furnishing of the City: No. 10. Allegorical Sculpture', *Town Planning Review*, Vol. 4 (2) pp. 95-97.

Adshead, S.D. (1913d) 'The Decoration and Furnishing of the City: No. 11. Utilitarian Furnishings', *Town Planning Review*, Vol. 4 (3) pp. 191-194.

Adshead, S.D. (1914a) 'The Decoration and Furnishing of the City: No. 12. Lamp Standards', *Town Planning Review*, Vol. 4 (4) pp. 292-296.

Adshead, S.D. (1914b) 'The Decoration and Furnishing of the City: No. 13. Tall Lighting Standards, Masts, and Car Poles,' *Town Planning Review*, Vol. 5 (1) pp. 47-48.

Adshead, S.D. (1914c) 'The Decoration and Furnishing of the City: No. 14. Shelters', *Town Planning Review*, Vol. 5 (2) pp. 139-140.

Adshead, S.D. (1914d) 'The Decoration and Furnishing of the City: No. 15. Refuges and Protection Posts', *Town Planning Review*, Vol. 5 (3) pp. 225-227.

Adshead, S.D. (1915) 'The Decoration and Furnishing of the City: No. 16. Trees', *Town Planning Review*, Vol. 5 (4) pp. 300-306.

Alberti, L.B. (1955) *Ten Books on Architecture*, (trns. Cosimo Bartoli (into Italian) and James Leoni (into English), London: Tiranti.

Alexander, C. *et al.* (1977) *Pattern Language*, Oxford: Oxford University Press.

Alexander, C. *et al.* (1987) *A New Theory of Urban Design*, Oxford: Oxford University Press.

Ambrose, P. and Colenutt, B. (1979) *The Property Machine*, Harmondsworth: Penguin.

Attoe, W. (1981) *Skylines: Understanding and Molding Urban Silhouettes*, New York: John Wiley and Sons.

Bacon, E. (1978) *Design of Cities*, London: Thames and Hudson.

Barnett, J. (1986) *The Elusive City: Five Centuries of Design, Ambition and Miscalculation*, London: The Herbert Press.

Beazly, E. (1967) *Design and Detail of Space Between Buildings*, London: Architectural Press.

Bentley, I. *et al.* (1985) *Responsive Environments: A Manual for Designers*, London: Architectural Press.

Birren, F. (1969) *Principles of Colour: A Review of Past Traditions and Modern Theories of Colour Harmony*, New York: Van Nostrand Reinhold.

Blowers, A. (1993) *Planning for a sustainable environment; a report by the Town and Country Planning Association*, London: Earthseen Publications.

Blumenfeld, H. (1953) 'Scale in Civic Design', *Town Planning Review*, Vol. XXIV, April, pp. 35-46.

Brand, K. (1992) *The Park Estate*, Nottingham: Nottingham Civic Society.

Brundtland, The World Commission on Environmental Development (1987) *Our Common Future*, Oxford: Oxford University Press.

Buchanan, D.A. and Huczynski, A.A. (1985) *Organisational Behaviour: An Introductory Text*, Englewood Cliffs: Prentice Hall.

Chevreul, M.E. (1967) *Principles of Harmony and Contrast of Colours* (1839) reprinted, Introduction and notes by F. Birren, New York: Van Nostrand Reinhold.

Collins, G.R. and Collins, C.C. (1986) *City Planning According to Artistic Principles*, New York: Random House.

Cullen, G. (1986) *The Concise Townscape*, London: Architectural Press.

Dewhurst, R.K. (1960) 'Saltaire', *Town Planning Review*, Vol. XXXI, July pp. 135-144.

Düttmann, M., Schmuck, F. and Uhl, J. (1981) *Colour in Townscape*, London: The Architectural Press.

Edwards, A.T. (1926) *Architectural Style*, London: Faber and Gwyer.

Elkin, T. and McLaren, D. (1991) *Reviving the City: towards sustainable urban development*, London: Friends of the Earth.

Gadbury, J. (1989) *A Sustainable Site for Development*, Park Residents Newsletter, No. 27, June 1992.

Geddes, P. (1949) *Cities in Evolution*, London: Williams and Norgate.

Gibberd, F. (1955) *Town Design*, 2nd Edition, London: Architectural Press.

Girourard, M. (1985) *Cities and People: A Social and Architectural History*, New Haven: Yale University Press.

Glancy, J. (1989) *New British Architecture*, London: Thames and Hudson.

Glancy, J. (1992) 'Gorblimey, Guv, all it needs is muffin men and sweeps', *The Independent*, 14th November.

Halprin, L. (1972) *Cities*, Cambridge, MS: MIT Press.

Hitler, A. (1971) *Mein Kampf*, translated by Ralph Manheim, Boston: Houghton Mifflin.

Hobhouse, H. (1975) *The History of Regent Street*, London: Macdonald and Jane's.

Howard, E. (1965) *Garden Cities of To-Morrow*, London: Faber.

Hughes, R. (1980) *The Shock of the New: Art and the Century of Change*, London: British Broadcasting Corporation.

Jacobs, J. (1965) *The Death and Life of Great American Cities*, Harmondsworth: Penguin.

Jencks, C. with Krier, L. (1988) 'Paternoster Square', *Architectural Design*, Vol. 58.(1/2) pp. VII-XIII.

Jencks, C. (1990) *The Language of Post-Modern Architecture*, London: Academy Editions.

Katz, D. (1950) *Gestalt Psychology*, New York: Ronald Press.

Koffka, K. (1935) *Principles of Gestalt Psychology*, London: Routledge and Kegan Paul.

Kostof, S. (1991) *The City Shaped: Urban Patterns and Meanings through History*, London: Thames and Hudson.

Kostof, S. (1992) *The City Assembled: The Elements of Urban Form Through History*, London: Thames and Hudson.

Krier, R. (1979) *Urban Space*, London: Academy Editions.

Krier, R. (1983) *Architectural Design Profile 49-Elements of Architecture*, London: AD Publications.

Le Corbusier, (1946) *Towards a New Architecture*, London: Architectural Press.

Le Corbusier, (1947) *Concerning Town Planning*, London: Architectural Press.

Le Corbusier (1967) *The Radiant City: Elements of a Doctrine of Urbanism to be used as the Basis of our Machine-Age Civilisation*, London: Faber.

Lenclos, J.P. (1977) 'France: How to Paint Industry', *Domus*, No. 568, March.

Lozano, E.E. (1974) 'Visual Needs on the Urban Environment', *Town Planning Review*, Vol. 45 (4) October, pp. 351-374.

Lynch, K. (1960) *The Image of the City*, Cambridge, MS: MIT Press.

Lynch, K. (1971) *Site Planning*, 2nd Edition, Cambridge, MS: MIT Press.

Lynch, K. (1972) *What Time is This Place?*, Cambridge, MS: MIT Press.

Lynch, K. (1981) *A Theory of Good City Form*, Cambridge, MS: MIT Press.

Maertens, H. (1884) *Der Optische Mastab in der Bildenden Kuenster*, 2nd Editon, Berlin: Wasmath.

Matthew, D. and Rodwell, A. (1991) *The Environmental Impact of the Car*, London: Greenpeace.

Morgan, B.G. (1961) *Canonic Design in English Medieval Architecture*, Liverpool: Liverpool University Press.

Morris, A.E.J. (1972) *History of Urban Form: Before the Industrial Revolution*, London: George Godwin.

Morris, A.E.J. (1994) *History of Urban Form Before the Industrial Revolution*, 3rd Edition, London: Longman.

Moughtin, J.C. (1992) *Urban Design: Street and Square*, London: Butterworth Architecture.

Mumford, L. (1938) *The Culture of Cities*, London: Secker and Warburg.

Mumford, L. (1944) *The Condition of Man*, London: Secker and Warburg.

Mumford, L. (1946) *City Development*, London: Secker and Warburg.

Mumford, L. (1961) *The City in History*, London: Secker and Warburg.

Mumford, L. (1968) *The Urban Prospect*, London: Secker and Warburg.

Murdock, N. (1984) 'The decline of the corner in Brussels', *Architecural Design*, Vol. 16 (4) pp. 124-126.

Myers, N. (1987) *The Gaia Atlas of Planet Management*, London: Pan.

Norberg-Schulz, C. (1971) *Existence, Space and Architecture*, London: Studio Vista.

Norberg-Schulz, C. (1980) *Genius Loci: Towards a Phenomenology of Architecture*, London: Academy Editions.

Owens, S. (1991) *Energy Conscious Planning*, London: CPRE.

Peets, E. (1927) 'Famous Town Planners. II. Camillo Sitte', *Town Planning Review*, Vol. 12 (4) pp. 249-259.

Pevsner, N. (1955) *The Englishness of English Art*, London: British Broadcasting Corporation.

Porter, T. (1982) *Colour Outside*, London: The Architectural Press.

Pugin, A.W.N. (1841a) *Contrasts*, Leicester: Leicester University Press, (reprinted 1969).

Pugin, A.W.N. (1841b) *The True Principles of Pointed or Christian Architecture*, London: Henry G. Bohn.

Rasmussen, S.E. (1969) *Town and Buildings*, Cambridge, MS: MIT Press.

Ravetz, A. (1980) *Remaking Cities: Contradictions of the Recent Urban Environment*, London: Croom Helm.

Rossi, A. (1982) *The Architecture of the City*, Cambridge, MS: MIT Press.

Scruton, R. (1979) *The Aesthetics of Architecture*, London: Methuen.

Serlio, S. (1982) *The Five Books of Architecture, An Unabridged Reprint of the English Edition of 1611*, New York: Dover Publications.

Sitte, C. (1901) *Der Stadte-Bau*, Wien: Carl Graeser and Co.

Smith, P.F. (1987) *Architecture and Harmony*, London: RIBA Publications.

Summerson, J. (1935) *John Nash, Architect to King George IV*, London: Allen and Unwin.

Summerson, J. (1963) *The Classical Language of Architecture*, Cambridge MS: MIT Press.

Tibbalds, F. (1992) *Making People-Friendly Towns*, London: Longman.

Tugnut, A. and Robertson, M. (1987) *Making Townscape, a contextual approach to building in an urban setting*, London: Mitchell.

Unwin, R. (1971) *Town Planning in Practice*, 2nd Edition, New York: B. Blom.

Venturi, R. (1966) *Complexity and Contradiction in Architecture*, New York: MOMA.

Vernon, H. (1962) *Principles of Architectural Form*, London: Allen and Unwin.

Vitruvius (1960) *The Ten Books of Architecture*, New York: Dover Publications.

Wölfflin, H. (1964) *Renaissance and Baroque*, London: Collins.

Zucker, P. (1959) *Town and Square*, New York: Columbia University Press.

INDEX